Another Time & Place

A Memoir in Verse

CHRIS GODDARD

"SILVERGHOST"

 FriesenPress

One Printers Way
Altona, MB R0G 0B0
Canada

www.friesenpress.com

Copyright © 2023 by Chris Goddard "Silverghost"
First Edition — 2023

All rights reserved.

No part of this publication may be reproduced in any form, or by any means, electronic or mechanical, including photocopying, recording, or any information browsing, storage, or retrieval system, without permission in writing from FriesenPress.

ISBN
978-1-03-915205-2 (Hardcover)
978-1-03-915204-5 (Paperback)
978-1-03-915206-9 (eBook)

1. POETRY, GENERAL

Distributed to the trade by The Ingram Book Company

DEDICATION

Many years ago, my father who enjoyed painting as a hobby suggested that I may enjoy painting as well. I did not think I had the ability or creativity to pursue painting.

I had begun writing poetry a few years earlier and had given him ten of my best works of poetry. He read them and took them to his workplace for his colleagues to read. He and his colleagues were quite impressed with my writing. My father said I had a gift and encouraged me to continue writing poetry; that was forty years ago.

This book of poetry is dedicated to him and my wife Lisa who continues to support my interest in writing poems.

Silverghost

TABLE OF CONTENTS

CHAPTER 1
ANOTHER TIME & PLACE

Though Another Time & Place 2
Another Time & Place 3
A gathering of friends 4
A lone being 5
A little part of me 8
A place once known revisited 9
A reason to be 12
A shining star still shines bright 13
A smile for all occasions; a kindness set apart ... 15
A picture of time 16
A gift 17
A gift of gold 18
A smile from within a heart 19
A thought 21
A voice; the spirit that moves 22
A voice more than words 24
Best friends 25
Eyes in the darkness 26
Feelings from the heart 27
For someone special 28
In her own special way 29
Just a moment of your time 30
Lesson one: patience, courage, and short hair 31
Ode to love still carried within 33
Special moments, there are so few 35
Something special found within 36

Something within 37
That feeling inside 38
That place called home 39
The one thing special 40
The spoken words through the eyes of a teacher 41
Upon the land I walked 43
Wordsworth 44
Where the magic lives 45

CHAPTER 2
SORROW

A time to reflect on what to expect 48
A pooh day 49
A moment in time 50
Beginning of the end 53
Dim reminder 54
Darkness, destiny, thoughts remain 56
Lost within truth, thought 58
Remembering those who we've lost 59
There's an emptiness within 60
To memories 61
Upon this day of sadness in our hearts 63
Without 64
The final chapter 65
The searching begins again 66

CHAPTER 3
HOW IT HAPPENED

A second ago 68
The book 69
Walled in 71
Environmentally sound; just a bubble 72

The walls of time 73
The Big Bang 75
When the grain elevator fell / The troop and the tower .. 77
Elevated to the edge 78
A path that leads a way 79
For the moment, then there was dust 81
No will or right 82
This too shall pass 84

CHAPTER 4
IMAGINATION

But a piece of paper, a thought 88
But a flicker of light 89
Letters of time 90
Me and my shadow 92
Mind games 94
Rhymes 96
Teaching a lesson learned and savoured again 98
Timeless simple truth 99
To touch the sky 100
A touch of green 101

CHAPTER 5
OBSERVATIONS

An idea? 104
To picture to place to relate 105
After the cold 106
Birds of flight 107
Belief 109
Garbage to end of the waste 110
How can I help? 112
It's good 114

Knowing the thought process 116
Rhymes and reasons, words of thought................117
Smoke gets in your eyes 119
The great shelving debates 121
The golf ball diving championship, a story inspired 122
The daily grind 124
Time flies 126
Yes, it's Monday morning again! 127
Worthwhile 129

CHAPTER 6
POINT OF VIEW

Beyond the forest 132
Far horizon 133
Keepers of the night................................134
The light within 136
So, few have known 137
Through changes 138
The captain 139
Where the spirit still lies.........................141
The write stuff.....................................142

CHAPTER 7
HISTORY

Darkened peace, souls release 144
Forgotten remains discovered 146
Keeper of the light, Hope Island 147
Life remnants remain 150
The lighthouse 152
Over the way once, the cow path leads 153
Over the way they came 155
Point of no return..................................156

River of life 157
Ruins of yesteryear, great ships lie beneath the waters .. 158
The chosen few 159
The past etched in stone 160
There stood a house 161
Where the river turns 162

CHAPTER 8
COVID-19 PANDEMIC

A path chosen for inspiration, a token 164
Waiting to get my shot in the arm 166
Come together right now six feet away 168
Foundations within a desire 171
When can I get a shot in the arm for real? 172
Getting a shot in the arm, the next day regrets 176
Isolation, how long will it last? 178
Still the movement now, 2020 180
What's next, 2022? 183
Return to sender 185
Volunteering a sense of pride 187

CHAPTER 9
REMEMBERING, HOW TO

Heaving spherical objects to target 190
Riding a bike; a renewed sensation 192
Spectacles through the looking glass 194
The love of snow, or just shoving it! 197
The ability to talk and not text 199

CHAPTER 10
IN THE DARK

A close encounter of an alien kind .202
As darkness filled the room, dark night. 205
Dark is the night. 207
It came in the night 208
Something in the mist. 210
The fire inside 213

CHAPTER 11
NORTH FOLK

Autumn leaves 216
A place once visited, these feelings are aware 218
Bala . . . a time not forgotten, 2020 220
The night before the Bala Cranberry Festival 222
Up North, Bala, a place to know. .224
Where the journey begins, the Bala way 226

CHAPTER 12
FAIRY TALES

The tooth fairy 230
When will the tooth fairy retire?. .232
Christmas cheer 234
The elusive Easter Bunny 236
Monkey business; twins 238
Night before Christmas. 239
Santa's helper 240
Walter 243

CHAPTER 13
KIDS

Another day in paradise; the cottage 246
A child, a lifetime, and experience .248
Bearing it all 251
A moment with Nate, for Matty. 253
Mr. Turtle. 255
Rhys: enthusiastic and confident 257
Sofija: the princess 260
Wide-eyed and smiles. 262
The elusive hidden creek 263

CHAPTER 14
INTO THE DEEP

295 feet; scuba diving 266
A world of its own 268
A gale in November; the **Edmund Fitzgerald** 269
Far below 271
Hello 272
Into the deep 275
Murphy's law of scuba diving 277
Outside looking in 279
Questions of the deep 282
The space within diving 284

CHAPTER 15
PEOPLE

A gift revealed many years to acquire. 288
A game of golf; the hazards of old age 289
A nun above us all; a very habitable character. 292
A splash of life. 295

Earl of Grey 297
Fair maiden 298
Maid Marian 299
Maiden journey 301
Hangry through the change's new insight 303
Humbled to the core; just kind of in limbo. 305
Sidekicks 307
Tanks, buddy; something you 'member pretty good.....308
Teaching; a learning experience 310
The guts, the glory; golf, it's just a game.................312
The par is part of the goal 315
'Twas the night before at the Lukasiks; a painting affair 317
The mystic man 319
The pride of one; the coach..............................321
The half-century club 322
Touchdown in the Enzone 323
Woody Tinder McSplinter................................325
Woodsy McTimber Stalwart: man of the forest 327
Through the looking glass; Les once more 329
Unmasking...the truth is revealed 330
The warming effect of foot bags........................332
Poly-gnomials..334
A connection with strings attached 336
This thing called love.....................................338
BBQed to a steak dinner 339
Les or more, it's pretty Coules 341

CHAPTER 16
CREATIVITY EXPLAINED

iPhone, I see the possibilities..........................344
Blackrock: a fishing tale as a kid 346
So the journey begins again renewed..................348

The early days back in school	350
The red fruit from A to Z	353
Paint by numbers; to the painter's place	355
Whirligig, whatchamacallit; you know what I mean?	357
A novel idea in the sixties to the present	359
Unique, up before you're discovered.	363
Life within a dream; the story continues	365
Breakfast of champions; retired, finally.	367
The three of us, explained	369
The milkman and the door in the wall	370
Cache Lake Annual Leaseholders' Regatta; the crab race	372
Cache Lake: a great escape	374
The beat of the drum falls silent, religiously	376
The Outhouse, in the great outdoors	378
Through the lens to the canvas	381
Thank Cod for Newfoundland	383
The rock by the sea, Newfoundland	385
Getting screeched in is a thing, just once	387
Lefthanded, leftovers & left behind	388
Looking for sunlight on a dreary day	390
Bitten by the Cache Lake Bee	392
Green effects	394
A visionary and spiritual advisor	396
The stinger is really a harpoon.	398
It happened one night	400
Gym.	402
The view through the looking glass, FaceTime	403
My first computer, a keyboard, and a ribbon	405
Along the cottage road, silverbirch beach, now silverbirch road	407
This place called home	409
Life in a box of crayons revealed	411

The air is thinner up there 412
Autumn in Bala ...A Lessened Year 2020..............414
Bala by the Bay...together again 2022................416
A means to write in verse 418
Falling signs......................................419
Traditions, the changing times at Bala...............421
Early to bed early to rise, I think? 423
The Mo I know......................................425
The Halloween pumpkin was great fully filled 427
The Ugly Stick a rhythmic delight....................429
Nuts..431
Losing my marbles..................................433
Looking at sheet of white paper? 435
Bed bugs...437
Just a matter of lines from still to life 438
Searching for buried treasure, X marks the spot 439
The Trail for buried treasure, part II..................441
My imagination went away 444
Searching for winter 446
Friesen Family 448
The next step, viewing from the other side, published ...450

CHAPTER 1
ANOTHER TIME & PLACE

A Memoir in Verse

THOUGH ANOTHER TIME & PLACE

Many years a writer, through ideas and thoughts,
Words in verse, the rhythm I had crossed.
Experience of mine that I have pursued,
Are printed in this book and a great read too.

These special poems selected with pride,
Another Time & Place to pursued.
Adventure in writing I'll let you decide,
In Loss and Sorrow this happens too.

How it happened, in Imagination explored,
Observations experienced and a Point of view.
·Though History in time and COVID pandemic exposed,
Remembering how to cope In the dark too.

The North folk adventures fantasy in Fairy tales,
Remembering as Kids searching into the deep.
The lives through People and Creativity explained,
These poems from the heart a special treat.

The lens of a camera seeing life change,
These poems are written from the heart.
My perspective through words, and experiences,
In Another Time & Place is just one part.

ANOTHER TIME & PLACE

You and I; two of a kind, intertwined.

Feeling of love is held within;
Feelings of sadness never end.
Loving someone as we should be;
Dealing with death wasn't for me.
Feelings of emptiness, not being there,
In a far-off place, without a care.
Lost inside in an empty space;
Caring for someone without a place.
It's hard to be two when one's not there;
Feeling alone, lost, and scared.
We were together; nothing ever mattered,
Now you're gone, my life is shattered.
A broken heart, dealing with pain;
Fresh from the start, beginning again.
Tears rolled down my face for you,
Wondering why I must live without you.
Just thinking in this empty place,
It's dark and cold without a trace.
Time continues; your life has ceased.
You're up in heaven in tranquility and peace.

A GATHERING OF FRIENDS

Now it's time; the moment draws near;
All who come for one who's here.
Carried within, for each has one;
A special time, this moment for one.

Upon their face, a smile appears;
With that moment does also a tear.
With saddened hearts, they come to pray,
For one so special is here today.

More than pain, more than sorrow;
A loss of a friend has no tomorrow.
So, they gather with their thoughts;
A moment of silence, the pain has brought.

When they leave, they will never forget,
With that moment for one has left.
Within a few years, some will return;
This very place, with deepened concern.

A LONE BEING

Within the blackness, the dawning of the night; within the silence, uttering no realm of time. The moment brief and unenduring; the stillness, though vast and inhibiting, overwhelms the darkness. The glitter of light dwarfed by the sea of tranquility, as the moment breed's form. This moment the soul finds the inner peace. A sense of no reality; through the night stillness, the simplicity, an insignificant time. A thought, a memory, a time of wonderment, where thoughts and ideas soar as an eagle whose flight has but one purpose: the endless search for life. The pursuit of freedom, where life and beauty are but one aspect of life.

This moment of desire, the wonderful bliss, with no regards, no pending problems, no distractions; a limitless sense of being and not yet totally alone. As each time it is read, new ideas and thoughts are revealed, new discoveries, new outlooks on life. As each aspect of this, the endless change, where desires are met like thoughts, the tears trickle down the page. Where the sense of wisdom, life's journey is fought, as the inner soul, whose thoughts search for freedom to rule. The innermost soul dominates as a feeling; the heart grows fond of love, this question that is unanswered. When the mind grows weary, the subconscious brings the meanings of dreams. The mind grows ever closer to that place. Each step is closer still as the lines, the words are meaningful, whereas the story changes. The warmth that leaves the body cold, drawing in the chill of the night. The grip of pain, the silent cry, the inner voice. Endless searching for that inner peace, silence, the unending, unwilling stillness. As life is but a frozen wasteland through the cries, echoes sound of distant voices from within the deep. That disconcerting look, a feeling of bewilderment, a sense of loss. In the blackness, where no one will know, no one can see you or hear you, you are still alone in the cold harsh reality of time. An endless façade, forward, onward still, within each second, the grains of sand displacing what lurks beneath. Within each second of time, different sounds, ideas, and thoughts. Each word, read once and not forgotten.

The stories told repeatedly by Grandpa, whose voice you remember so well. The rise, fall, and pitch; your little girl fantasies hanging on every word. Whose deep voice sometimes resonates the fond memories in each aspect, now seemingly vast, as waves on distant shores. The smell of burning wood fills every crevice of your existence. Your mind eagerly listening with utter enjoyment, relishing the moment as the juice from a sweet orange, savouring each drop as if it were the last. This wide-eyed little schoolgirl whose expectations far surpassed her ideas. Whose ideas and inner strength grew as did the memories. A pair of red shoes, adoringly loved and cared for, grew as did her special qualities. Her uniqueness, her warmth and inner strength, a sense of love that comes from within. Whose compassion and vitality transcend all others, whose belief in her exceeds expectations. Whose softened voice often heard now echoes in your mind as only just yesterday. As time, there is little space for another within, one heart there is one more. Now, some years later, has been told. As the stories, the memories, the dimly lit candle flickers in the wind, almost translucent of life. The wax, now softened over time, is all but gone. Within the light, the once soft hand now withered as the winds on a barren plain. The lines and wrinkles, the highways of life, tracing a pattern whose meaning tells all a story.

Still caresses the pen, on the dimly lit page. A splash of ink and thoughts fill the once empty lines, steadily and briskly as not to forget, in finest detail of being.

At dusk, the eve of darkness embellishes the inner soul, the howl, the haunting echoes, a voice once passed these ears. The decades of individuals, and friends, who have now passed on. Their memories, the pictures, now darkened and faded, the corners bent, were once proudly placed but are now worn. As the photos, if they could speak, to those energetic sounds that are the promise of life surpassed, to those who now are remembered. Many years together, whose smiles resonate in the minds of the young, in thoughts. The vision of those now reminisced, a sweetened smile now with saddened face, withered and aged. When the ink dries, this parchment will be a testament of time yet forgotten. This one being, and always alone, is now and forever silenced.

A LITTLE PART OF ME

So little of me I seem to share
To the ones so close who are not aware.
Understanding, knowledge, gentleness begins;
Gestures of kindness still flow within.
Things I care, I sometimes show;
Mystery of me, I really don't know.
The one I have seen, this one I care,
Though times like this, she's not aware.
So special, she is unable to meet;
A chance of life, a time of need.
Time of romance, so little of chance;
One so special, lost in a trance.
This one I care, she doesn't know,
What to say and how to show.
A chance perhaps, it may not last;
Hold on tight, hold on fast.
What to do, where to see within;
This is where the mystery begins.

A PLACE ONCE KNOWN REVISITED

Dawn arose, all around a hazy day;
Clouds darkened, soon changed to grey.
The wind blew cold, chilled to the bone;
Walking down the path, you're not alone.

A flashlight you have, lights the way,
Suddenly goes dark, so far away.
The rain has fallen, soaked to the bone;
Following the old path, far from home.

A phone you have, no signal in sight;
Down, into the forest, fear ignites.
The sky is black, once grey now green;
Wind blows stronger, uncertain you seem.

The forest ahead, the way unclear;
The path once remembered, was it here?
A light in the distance, eerie feeling within;
Slowly, you follow it, noises begin.

Over the bridge, it creaks and moans;
Steady under foot, you're not alone.
Upon each step, boards fall away;
Hesitation within, to go or stay.

The rain that fell ceased to fall;
The winds blew, now, not at all.
Feeling inside now, you're from here;
Each step taken; the path is clear.

Rain has gone, dampness in the air;
Searching for a path, barely there.
Up the hill and over the rise,
Hidden from sight, unrecognized.

The darkness, for once a light;
In forest, from once so bright.
Thickened trees, life that thrived;
Many years, the love, a family was alive.

For the cabin, hidden away;
The path that follows, a gate leads a way.
The gate that blocks is worn and grey;
The path once worn is hidden today.

Upon the porch, withered and worn,
Paint now blistered, shredded, and torn.
Light through the planks is seen,
Weather cracked and dotted with green.

Now, the screen, the door ajar;
Vacant and empty, distant by far.
Broken front door, a path leads;
Vast, darkened, yet destined to breathe.

Through the door, the way is clear;
Few passed, the warmth was here.
In the room, now dark and cold,
Lifeless, barren, not even a soul.

One step, boards creak and moan;
Each step taken; years have known.
Now hidden within shadows, lost inside;
Time has passed for those once tried.

*Thick cobwebs hang in the air;
The smell lingers, damp and bare.
Now each step is lost within time;
The silence echoes a step at a time.*

A REASON TO BE

There's a feeling inside, it's not allowed;
It cannot be shared or spoken now.
No one can see it, or even be heard;
No expression of voice to utter those words.

A loss of voice, a feeling within;
It's carried each day it begins.
In the silence, a cry for relief;
Perhaps one day a chance believes.

Though buried within, it cannot run free;
No means of voice, no reason to be.
All the while, it's locked inside;
The day will come you're able to try.

The struggle waged; feelings are there,
To find the meaning, dazed, unaware.
Hidden from sight, from where it begins;
Searching for a way inside, it lies within.

Yet a moment one will see,
The voice within, a reason to be.
A place to voice, the journey begins;
Perhaps, one day, the healing wins.

A SHINING STAR STILL SHINES BRIGHT

There's one soul I've come to know;
Many years she's done and more.
Joy that she shares, above all she cares;
Still there is a lot, even more.
The spirit that's stored, hidden, and absorbed,
Where smiles can always be found.
Wait a moment or two, amazing the view;
They gather when she is around.
A shining star, still shining so far;
This light will never go out.
Maureen's understanding, thoughts, aiding the distraught,
She cares when the love flows out.
With resources and tools, and God-given rules,
The courage to find and discover.
Through the spoken words, many years have been heard;
This trait, there is no other.
With new skills acquired, her passion and desire;
This experience is created and deserved.
Surprising new ways, she creates and displays,
A treasure to describe without words.
Looking through the lens, many hours she spends,
To observe the world and behold.
To focus and project, this world she'll protect,
For the photo once gifted takes hold.
A passion for life, take hold and delight;
This feeling may never be sold.
The warmth Maureen shares, above all she shares,
This love will always take hold.

One spirit, one soul, many years we've been told,
This love and life are free.
Take this time, make each moment shine;
This day, I make this decree.

A SMILE FOR ALL OCCASIONS; A KINDNESS SET APART

As for the silence, at times it abounds,
Yet bubbly and buoyant when others surround.
There is warmth that's carried within;
It's found inside from where it begins.

Yet sometimes when life goes wrong,
She faces the problem, for inside she's strong.
As for the trials that life gives us,
Lisa tries her best and never gives up.

At times she's quiet and not saying a word,
For she is sweet, and the kindness deserves.
Though her words, she often speaks;
For, as her hubby, what a wondrous treat.

As for her task, in her skill she displays,
For she's neat and tidy in her own special way.
Though often smiling, the least of her frowns,
For cumbersome the job here, smiles abound.

Always tidy, there's never a mess;
She's a special person, no one would guess.
As for her allergies, they're always there;
As for the dust, it doesn't seem to care.

She is special, so few are aware;
As for a friend, she's one who cares.
As for her pride, she's nothing to prove;
Lisa has everything and nothing to lose.

A PICTURE OF TIME

Frozen in time, memories of mine;
The time for now has ceased.
The picture lives, the memory forbids,
Whose time has changed the least.

A forgotten face, hard to replace;
Time seems to have taken away.
A piece of time, a picture in mind,
Whose memories won't go away.

Void of space, of time, and place;
All ideas seem to freeze.
No day to wage, no time taken away;
All life seems to cease.

Frozen within, no time begins;
Life seems ill at ease.
A treasure within, a memory begins;
Life is still at peace.

No time does age, no life takes away,
What till then still strong.
No worries, no wrongs, all seem calm;
Nothing for now has gone.

A GIFT

An ability by choice,
In ways to voice.
Words a means to talk,
Chosen words.

A means of verse,
A beginning, a point of thought.
An idea has brought,
Feelings, a thought.

Expression, a meaning through words,
A form of art.
Emotions of the heart,
Within a voice to be heard.

Years to progress,
A verse, no less.
Ideas within a new light,
A vision not seen.

Versatility, a means,
Words, an ability to write.
To be aware,
All that is there.

To view as others go by,
To observe in ways.
To speak in ways,
Expression, a voice that thrives.

A GIFT OF GOLD

Perhaps for one, the freedoms come;
A change, a moment now free.
With the time, the moment in mind,
The freedom, the ability, now believed.

Within her hand, a change of plans;
Within her mind, a change.
For now, it seems, in her dreams,
A fight, her time, her change.

Upon the walls, the colour dissolves;
New life is beginning again.
Now, set in gold, so begins her goal;
Time and courage and strain.

As the days they begin to wage,
Each piece is placed in time.
Soon, perhaps her goal, at last,
Will stand the test of time.

Within that mind, the moment shined,
For all will come to see.
Within, there's one who struggled to become;
This moment, a time is believed.

The final goal, a gift of gold,
The light that shines on through.
Now your place, a change of space;
Now you have something to prove.

A SMILE FROM WITHIN A HEART

There's one for whom all succumbed;
This one she is special to know.
In that she shares, above all, she cares;
She's special, she's one, and she knows.

Within her heart, one love, now a part;
A feeling, a caring, she shows.
Within, she warns, she shares and warms;
This love to each she shows.

Through her eyes, the story still lies;
The story has yet to be told.
Within just one, the caring has won;
The mystery for now unfolds.

Within her voice, she's chosen by choice,
She and more than most.
Denise is but one so few who will succumb,
As others who are so close.

Within this soul, where love takes hold,
This life is hard for some.
Yet she strives, her will survives;
Her love and pride have won.

When she shares the love, she cares,
In all she's come to know.
Carried within, this love begins;
In time, she will begin to show.

And yet to some, to each there's one;
Within her story is now told.
As each now grows, they shape and mould;
Their lives and love unfold.

May you always strive from what you know;
It's in your heart you find it will grow.

A THOUGHT

To give a thought cost nothing at all;
It's a part of caring; it's within us all.
More precious than gold, money cannot buy;
It's a part of you, the part that tries.
It comes from within and carries on out,
To a friend in need, a soul in doubt.
It's something beautiful that one can share,
To show your feelings, to show you care.
It can go on forever or be so brief;
It can last a lifetime or be so free.
It tells them all the ways you feel,
And that it is true: thoughts are real.

A VOICE; THE SPIRIT THAT MOVES

It happened one night long ago,
Was on the night, I remembered it so.
The night was cold, yet so clear;
No voice, no sound, and yet it's here.

The sky was dark, no moon, no stars,
No lights, no one, yet beyond afar.
Beyond the water, so cold out here,
Not a ripple seen, for it was near.

Yet only once and never again,
Though never perhaps or will it end.
For on that night, asleep, I awoke;
There was a voice here, it spoke.

No one around, no one in sight;
No lights to see within a fright.
Yet all alone, still unafraid;
The voice that spoke having little to say.

To only you, no one else;
So look beyond, within thy self.
You will find the spirit that heals;
So look within the light reveals.

Within a voice, a choice of words;
Thou, you will choose within a verse.
The path is smooth and worn down bare;
It's the other one, the one that cares.

Then it was dark, the voice was gone;
Perhaps the light, it has moved on.
With the wind that began to blow;
With that voice, now no one knows.

A VOICE MORE THAN WORDS

There is a voice that means so much,
Perhaps even more than it is to touch.
It's in the power, a voice through words,
A voice that listens, a voice that's heard.

A voice that's caring, soft-spoken words,
Familiar to the sounds, so warming when heard.
Within each word, the emotions surround,
A sense more than feelings, warmth is around.

Something that's felt it caring from within,
Perhaps just to speak, so the feeling begins.
To ease the pain, a voice that is not,
Freely of speech, encouragement has brought.

There is a feeling that's carried within,
It's shared with others, it starts, it begins.
It's found inside, where the warmth consoles,
Shared with others, the one who knows.

To call on the phone, to listen, to hear;
The rhythmic sound resonates in here.
More than a text, more than a thought;
A moment for someone special has brought.

This time of year, we all need a friend,
A moment to laugh, some time to lend.
Take a moment, take some time,
It will resonate back and make you shine.

BEST FRIENDS

For there is but only one,
For few there really are.
And those who have just one,
They are special by far.

All our lives, we struggle,
For that in which we hope.
The one that we can share,
In that we learn to cope.

Someone we don't really know,
Special feelings we can share.
Learning is more than a feeling;
Accepting is how we really care.

For those of us who strive,
To find that which we know.
In our lives, there is only one,
In that we learn to grow.

Perhaps for those who cannot find,
The special ones, they need.
To find there is only one choice,
To look within is to believe.

EYES IN THE DARKNESS

*Within her eyes, hidden by surprise,
A story has yet to be told.
Though many have tried to reveal this side,
No one will ever know.*

*The mystery revealed, the story concealed,
The book is almost closed.
To place a mark, idea embarked,
Only the reader really knows.*

*A thought to grasp, ideas at last;
All seems black and white.
The story soon ends, mystery expands,
The story another will write.*

*Where to begin a mystery within,
Knowledge not really known.
For in her eyes, the story still lies,
Lost forever in the poem.*

FEELINGS FROM THE HEART

When you are feeling alone,
No friends by your side,
You're not alone;
We're all in God eyes.

Sadness changes to pain,
Tears fall like rain.
The pain you're feeling inside;
This never dies.

The heart grows fond,
You feel you can't go on.
You're torn apart,
Feeling from the heart.

The pain goes on;
Heartache grows strong.
You want to cry;
You can't and don't know why.

You've lost your best friend;
You think it's the end.

FOR SOMEONE SPECIAL

So, you are down and feeling blue;
Here's a message to see you through.
You're in our thoughts and on our minds;
It's not the same; we hope you are fine.

Perhaps a thought may bring a smile,
That special something for a little while.
Those of us, we, us, we are aware;
We wish you well; we really care.

As a friend and more than some;
For it is remembered and it's become.
As a smile, it's always there;
When you're around and so you share.

With each moment, another arrives;
As each day, a new surprise.
At this time, a smile appears,
With that thought, that feeling nears.

For this thought, a surprise for you;
This day had brought a birthday wish too.
As the warmth, it will be shared,
With the hope it'll always be there.

In this thought, and now you smile,
You've got the knack; you've got the style.
With each day, you will carry within,
From here it starts; in here it begins.

IN HER OWN SPECIAL WAY

She brings a smile, and the warmth she shares;
It comes from the heart, so few are aware.
She cares in her own special way,
Perhaps not spoken; that is her way.
Within her voice, a softness set apart,
Known only by some; she cares from the heart.
She brings laughter, at times breaking a smile;
Though serious at times, for that is her style.
There are few like her, no one I've ever met;
It's in the knowing, not knowing, what to expect.
She could talk for hours, without taking a breath;
Times hanging on every word, waiting for the next.
She holds you in suspense, in just a small part;
Brings a tear to your eye, laughter in your heart.
Holding on every word, taking laughter within;
Without breaking a smile, her serious wins.
There are few stories, few have never read,
Stories different, kinds have yet to be said.
Within her eyes, still a world unknown,
A hidden surprise, where friendships have grown.
A special lady, for few will ever know;
Nancy is one, she is special, and she knows.

JUST A MOMENT OF YOUR TIME

A reader of poetry you do not have to be;
To understand is the language, you do, indeed.
To speak just English is a task on its own;
You do it well and you're not alone.
To grasp just a thought and it's perceived,
You've done that well; do you not agree?
So simple is the idea, the riddle isn't hard;
The rhyme is the tale, it's in the learning by far.
So few who understand, who can grasp just one;
You've done this well; you have now become.
One of so few who can think and see,
Who doesn't snicker, shun, or disagree.
A final thought, for my time is so brief,
This time well spent and more than a need.
If you cannot accept or will not concede,
I will understand, for I will take heed.
The last this will be, and thanks for the space;
Time now remembered in another time and place.

LESSON ONE: PATIENCE, COURAGE, AND SHORT HAIR

Stop, think, relax, eyes ahead;
Feet set apart and drop the head.
Relax the body, shoulders at rest;
Bend the knees, remember what's next.

Watch the leaf and follow through;
Swing the club, you've got the moves.
Poised on the green, she sets the scene;
Eyes focused downward upon the green.

A last prayer before the swing;
To hit the ball, the final thing.
The hair falls upon the face;
A distorted vision, a loss of pace.

The crucial swing, the ball is ablaze;
The object soars just ten feet away.
Nancy's smile and a shining face;
Within, a laugh, the pride takes face.

With a moment, a broken smile;
The ball did soar not a mile.
Up and beyond, up to the sky;
Towards the trees, in the grass, it'd lie.

To the right and far away;
Perhaps a second, stay calm and pray.
So many clubs, so many swings;
To fight the right, the club will sing.

Set and poise to calm the nerves;
Away the club, her pride was hurt.
Countless swings, the ball would fly;
Not nearer the flag, the ball did lie.

Neither closer to right, nor the left;
Better off putting, no ill regrets.
Examine the green, the slope to lie;
Beyond the strokes, a sense of pride.

The ball was hit and rolled on past;
The cup did lie beyond her grasp.
More than once, she was displeased;
Patience, practise was all she'd need.

Perhaps just eight, or was it nine?
Just one putt, this moment she shined.
Beyond the holes was patience and time;
Eager to improve her skills refined.

The final hole, the last, indeed;
The score perhaps beyond degree.
A day of fun, a time away;
This game of golf for one did play.

Beyond the trees, gullies, and creeks,
Over marshes and traps, occasional shriek.
The greatest swing, with patience and poise;
This game is fun, yet still annoys.

ODE TO LOVE STILL CARRIED WITHIN

Many years it has been, one love in my dreams;
For time has passed me by.
All that I have dreamed each day it seems;
The love of my life is by my side.

Lost in thought, emptiness has brought,
Where to go from here?
As my mind races of so many places;
I am lost and full of tears.

The silence still looms, lost in gloom,
My ability just to move.
All that makes me whole, now an empty soul;
Nothing more can I lose.

Where smiles glowed, tears now flow;
Memories so many now stored.
A fleeting smile, eerie feeling all the while;
This place lost forever more.

The years once grasped, lost in the past,
In the hours, months, and days.
A photograph or two, once cherished mood;
She is in a happier place, I pray.

The sounds that I hear, a voice so near,
Laughter once echoed in this place.
Memories once shared, barely there,
Where laughter once filled this space.

A photograph, once displayed, now worn fades;
The corners, the edges, frayed.
Faces and scenes, memories of once been;
A picture just vanishes away.

Now scenes of grey darken each day,
Colours of black and white.
Where emptiness reigns, the endless pain,
My ability to find what is right.

SPECIAL MOMENTS, THERE ARE SO FEW

Within my thoughts, I think of her;
Within my voice, I hear the words.
With each moment, there was the time;
With her voice, a new light shined.
Within the warmth, there was a glow;
When she was around, I felt it flow.
Within my words, the feelings change;
When she was here, the warmth remained.
To hold a hand, the warmth surrounds;
The feeling back, there are no bounds.
With a walk, a simple pleasure;
Within that time, one must treasure.
Cherished moments, there were so few;
Remembering the ones will carry you through.
You must be strong in times of doubt;
You live and learn what life is about.

SOMETHING SPECIAL FOUND WITHIN

It is to remember, it is to recall,
The memories, perhaps, for one and all.
As the days, there were so few;
The weeks were short, for that I knew.
At the dawn, the day begun;
Lost in the darkness, the moment for one.
Within the darkness there came a light;
It brightened the mood and changed the night.
It spoke with a voice, it spoke in rhymes,
It spoke of ideas, all different kinds.
It shared one thing, it shared above all,
It shared from within, it cared above all.
Perhaps, as a friend, is what appeared;
It moved in close and had no fear.
All it shared, all it showed;
It had a heart, it wasn't cold.
The things it shared, and most of all,
A friendship passed, it remembers and recalls.
As that moment, and many more,
It shared from beneath, like never before.

SOMETHING WITHIN

Deep within the soul inside,
There is an ache that is alive.
It hurts the one you care about most,
The one within who feels so close.
To speak of voice, expressions so real;
It's what's inside, the way you feel.
A loss of feeling, a loss of touch;
A loss of sense is all too much.
Within these words, within the voice,
The ones who act, chooses by choice.
Who will not speak or will not act?
He keeps it within and loses track.
No means to share the burden within,
A loss of vision, the hurt begins.
Perhaps a tear and hurt inside,
A loss of control, a loss to try.
Unable to hold, no means to reason;
A loss of feeling, something to believe in.
A soul to reach, a friend who shares,
To show the burden, someone who cares.

THAT FEELING INSIDE

It warms the heart, fills the soul;
The sensation inside, it takes a hold.
It fills the moments, hours, each day,
It cannot be broken or washed away.
It fills a lifetime growing each day;
It never weakens or fades away.
You carry it with you each day of your life;
You cherish each moment and each new life.
With that bond within others can share;
It comes from the heart, everyone is aware.

THAT PLACE CALLED HOME

Perhaps a thought may bring a smile;
That special someone for a little while.
All the while, may it bring even more;
That special touch, what it's looking for.
When you return and when you recall,
That place called home, it's special, above all.
With many friends, and more than some,
You are remembered, and you will become.
As your smile, it's always there;
You are around and always share.
With each moment, another arrives;
As each new day, a new surprise.
This day has brought a change for you;
As the warmth, may it be shared too.
With the hope it'll always be there,
And with another, it must be shared.
Now for a thought, for now you smile;
You've got the knack, you've got the style.
And with each day, you'll carry within,
For here it starts, and here it begins.

THE ONE THING SPECIAL

There is only one,
In that most of all.
It's found within;
Special, most of all.

Each is something different,
To each is only known.
For each is something special,
Within each that it's shown.

There is something special;
No two are alike.
No two share the same,
From within, brought to life.

It's when to know when,
The time is only right.
Something within itself;
You know when it's right.

Each has a special gift;
Years we may not know.
To discover our true calling,
Spread your wings, let it flow.

THE SPOKEN WORDS THROUGH THE EYES OF A TEACHER

As the moment, a voice appeared;
An introduction, for all to hear.
When she spoke, the sounds grew strong;
She spoke of kindness where all belonged.
She spoke of places so far away;
She spoke of home, a place to stay.
With that smile lights up the room,
She shared the light and abolished the gloom.
It is to remember, it is to recall,
The memories perhaps for one and all.
As the days, there were so few;
With the moments came something new.
Within the darkness, there came a light;
You brightened the mood and changed the night.
Andrea spoke with voice; you spoke of times;
She spoke of things, all different kinds.
She shared one thing, you shared above all,
She shared from within, she cared above all.
All you shared, for all you showed,
You had a heart, it wasn't cold.
Things you shared and most of all,
A friendship passed, remember, and recalled.
As that moment, and for many more,
You shared from beneath, as before.
For your kindness, though it was sweet,
A hidden smile would never defeat.
The warmth you brought was made aware;
These moments remembered and what you shared.

As the smile, that sparkle within,
That special something changed from within.
A smiling face, and you appeared,
From in the distance, and you were here.
As the light many times it appears,
With the soul the warmth is near.
With this day, may there be many more.
A spoken word, with exceptional rewards.

UPON THE LAND I WALKED

I wish to walk upon the ground,
To feel my own two feet.
I wish to climb upon the stairs,
The help I wish them free.
I wish to feel the sand below,
And walk upon the beach.
I wish to feel my own ten toes,
The land a place to reach.
I wish to feel my own two legs,
Rise up to the sky.
I wish to stand out there alone;
Perhaps one day I'll fly.
I wish they all could see me now,
My ability that I have reached.
I wish to teach them all someday,
Within my soul I've reached.
I wish they'd see it's really me,
This chair I cannot leave.
I wish to run, to walk, to jog;
I wish to be just be me.
I wish upon a star each night;
Each day I'm closer still.
I wish someday to find a way,
To ease my broken will.

WORDSWORTH

A voice enounced and spoke with finesse,
Systematically and grammatically correct.
And with red pen so began to abuse,
What is and what was, this wouldn't do.
Within the voice, and so often heard,
The beat of eight is what was deserved.
Within a few words, the future seemed grim;
So it arrived, and here it begins.
Within the silence, the thoughts appeared;
The voice of reason no longer was here.
With the magic, the voice was gone;
The will to create just didn't belong.
Within the sadness, that voice that spoke,
Driving the dagger into his cloak.
As the pain, the beat soon hushed;
The tragedy of it all was just too much.
With a last breath, the voice that spoke,
A final goodbye was suddenly invoked.
As the blood soon changed to black,
The ink had ceased this final attack.
Upon the paper, for now it's read,
Perhaps not a poet, was what she said.

WHERE THE MAGIC LIVES

For what is found and what is believed,
These special moments inside of me.
For what we share and times alone,
For what we've learned, our time has grown.
Newfound interests, each moment would lend,
In the days passed, might never end.
With each new day, another to come,
The magic was shared, especially for one.
A sense of hope, a new surprise;
We grew together, it changed our lives.
For someone special, in that we've found;
For now, we've grown, and it's allowed.
Within the hope, with these souls;
Within just one, it's always to know.
Within the smiles, within just one;
As our memories, they have begun.
Within a moment, for just a few;
For what was found, our friendship grew.
What is gained and what belongs,
A sense of magic that dearly belongs.
Perhaps the days, the ones to come,
The struggle, a challenge, to overcome.
As our time, each day we've grown;
As for the future, the light is known.
As for the path, this way is clear;
The road that turns, a change appears.
As the direction, it's what we chose,
For right or wrong, we cannot lose.
Perhaps a sign, perhaps once again,

To find the magic, perhaps only then.
Within a promise, within just one,
Within the truth, the strength for some.
A moment, a thought, if not for you;
The gift of love, refreshing and new.
To the memories and the love that she gives;
For this, the moment, where the magic lives.

CHAPTER 2
SORROW

A TIME TO REFLECT ON WHAT TO EXPECT

As the moments pass, a time to grasp,
A feeling not quite known.
A choice now taken, not forsaken,
A challenge for now has grown.
Now for the test, gains great respect;
The feeling is not yet known.
The task at hand, the blood will demand;
The outcome in days has grown.
The course is clear, and what was feared;
My life has changed for now.
A time to reflect and what to expect;
The chosen must take a vow.
The meter will take, to have and forsake;
The levels of sugar will abound.
The outcome now feared, pain draws near;
The changes inside now found.
The meter of choice, to reflect the voice;
The feeling is yet unknown.
The spear will poke, a painful jolt,
To blood now red has grown.
Upon the strip, the meter will dip;
The needle's colour now reigns.
The results are chosen, feelings are frozen;
The hourly regiment of pain.
Each day of my life, now filled with strife;
The choices a must to survive.
The sugars now rule, can be cruel;
I gain support to stay alive.

A POOH DAY

A day of pooh, yet some who knew,
Like me and you, I never knew.
Perhaps I am sad and almost glad,
At times I am mad, a moment I had.
I once was small and not even tall;
In darkness I would feel sad most of all.
The darkness reigns, though I never complain;
There is no one to blame for feelings I cannot explain.
Now all seems grey as each passing day,
Too weak to say I am still here today.
I know I am right, my will to fight;
My blessed plight to see the light.
Sounds that I hear, the pain I fear;
I am still here, glad that you are near.
The love is found, and friendships surround;
The warmth abounds when God is around.
With my holy cross, I am not lost;
This path will not stop, this is all for not.
Today, we must pray, the rosary to say;
One miracle to stay, the ability to walk away.
This saddens my heart to be yet apart;
The journey will start, I am afraid of the dark.
One day, a sign, a message of mine;
A blessed time, my eternal light will shine.

A MOMENT IN TIME

There was a time,
That comes to mind,
A time not long ago.
When one did see,
A vision to believe,
So fair and young and bold.

Beauty to behold,
A thought took hold,
A vision he could not part.
So beautiful this face,
One could embrace,
For love beheld his heart.

For, alas,
A chance to grasp,
A love he could not let go.
He had to see,
A chance to be,
For fear she would soon go.

At times, he tried,
Feelings he'd hide;
This love, he had to wait.
In time to know,
This love would show;
Many days he'd have to debate.

So real, so fair,
He could not bare,
To see what he had seen.
Alas, he tried,
To bare inside,
A chance to live a dream.

No ways to change,
His plans changed;
Commitment dashed his dates.
He couldn't go through,
This love, he knew,
This was the end of his fate.

A chance to see,
Again, to be,
To see her with his eyes.
Though just to be,
A vision to see,
Forever in his eyes.

Time had passed,
He wished he'd asked,
Just one more chance to grasp.
A chance to be,
This love, he's seen,
Forever he wishes was dashed.

*He's not insane,
It's not in vain,
A friend he is crazy about.
Too long it's been,
He hasn't seen,
This love, he doesn't doubt.*

BEGINNING OF THE END

Happiness dies,
A voice cries.
Tear on a face,
A lonely place.
All was fine,
Until a time.
Happening so fast,
It did not last.
Something so brief,
Changed to grief.
Feeling had died,
Happening and why.
She was here,
A sense of fear.
And now she's gone,
In heaven she belongs.
Without a word,
Silence is heard.

DIM REMINDER

As the light seems to fade,
Within warmth, it drifts away.

Now the light is almost out;
A single light is doused.

Sounds of voice have all gone;
Hushed are voices, emptiness belongs.

Echoes of laughter-filled, happy souls,
What of time, where did it go?

As now, the silence rings aloud.
What of us, what happens now?

The music within the souls has died.
Lost is the hope, as one did try.

The final flicker from once a light,
Now a dim glow, two souls did ignite.

A silence, hush, now rings aloud.
Where is the noise, for silence echoes now?

A trail of smoke breaks the night;
Darkness surrounds in taking its life.

As the eyes they seem to close;
Arise the music as silence goes.

For in the light, now I see;
Darkness now a likeness to be.

To awake now or will I dream.
Will I remember this place and scene?

Is this a dream I would like to try?
For in my mind a timeless sigh.

For all is black, no silence do I hear.
Now it's just one now, I fear.

COVID is done;
Welcome everyone.

DARKNESS, DESTINY, THOUGHTS REMAIN

Though times like now, mixed emotions within;
Uncertainty, oh, where it's to begin.
The first question it is to ask,
The answer though unable to grasp.
To place a call, thoughts of delight;
Disappointment to ponder, reasons despite.
So many questions, few answers are found;
The voice begins without hearing a sound.
To think, wonder, to ponder aloud;
Situations though possible, what happens now!
A call is placed, nervous yet scared;
Stumbling through words, the voice is aware.
Regrets and dismay, though happiness tries;
Within that moment, destiny still lies.
The number is dialled, but is it too late?
A voice appears, the machine soon plays.
A message is left, lost and dismayed;
A second is placed, one number at a time.
Who sits and waits to try to unwind?
Emotions stirred, now worried, he waits,
The answer still lies, the question he debates.
As the night is long and sleep is lost,
Morning soon comes, all ideas are crossed.
The day moves on, he sits and ponders;
Is he a fool as he waits and wonders?
The days turns to night, no call, no voice;
The decision to call, he is decided by choice.
One by one, thoughts soon appear,

Situations, answers, none that he hears.
His time but one the other to wait;
Destiny and darkness, disappointment debates.
Thoughts enter the mind, he talks aloud;
The weekend has passed many days now.
A question arose, in every conceivable way,
He tried to reason; thoughts took them away.
The time waits for the one who can reason,
One who shall decide, answers are pleasing.
The feeling lies deep within the soul,
Consuming the time, for he is not whole.
Feeling unhurried, plunder, the heart;
Waiting and watching, wanting to be apart.
For time it seems this is the one,
The timing still holds one to one.
Happiness and peace shall never become,
The soul's uncertainty will never be one.
Perhaps that voice may never come;
The time spent alone is strong for some.

LOST WITHIN TRUTH, THOUGHT

Through signs of life were not aware,
Lost within truth, the minds unaware.
A loss of tough feelings, without words;
No means to fight emotions undeserved.
Deep within dreams, trapped within thoughts;
Who wonders within true feeling forgot?
Who looks and listens, watches and stares?
Watching and waiting for truth beware.
Looking, searching, and hoping to find,
The truth within, the truth in time.
Something is seen, it's not there;
The answer to reason, certainty unfair.
The belief in something not really seen;
Not aware, lost within the dream.
Hoping and searching, looking for truth;
He searches within, trapped within his youth.
For silence will fall, yet undisturbed;
Hesitations, no signs, uttering no words.
The moment, the right, there will be a sign;
The words, the truth, understand in time.

REMEMBERING THOSE WHO WE'VE LOST

Though it may be a time of sadness,
The ones who cannot be with friends.
They are the ones we pray for,
Wishing we could see them again.

Some of us are together,
While others are apart.
It's being with the ones we care for;
Knowing it in our hearts.

Some of us are alone now,
With friends who have passed on.
We struggle to continue;
The pain inside grows strong.

It's our friends we miss,
Though try as we may.
We try to carry on;
The pain won't go away.

Times have passed on;
We wish they were around.
Now all is left in silence,
Not a word or even a sound.

THERE'S AN EMPTINESS WITHIN

Something I cannot control,
A feeling that won't let go.
There is a need, a feeling that yearns;
I don't know why or where to turn.
Times I feel as if I've died,
Only to reach out, I wish to try.
Seems I am lost within only words;
Gradually it seems to get worse.
I am shaking inside, don't know why;
I cry out, I am lost inside.
The feeling within, I cannot shake;
It haunts me when I am awake.
A dream a friend, I have lost my love;
In happiness, perhaps of what was.
There's a sadness in my heart;
Something's lost that is apart.
Perhaps and now, I am unable to feel,
A part of me that was so real.
Something inside now has died;
The loss I feel I cannot lie.
Within this feeling, there is hope,
Helping me deal, my ability to cope.
There is one who speaks who knows,
Within just a hug, the warmth controls.
Hold on tight, never let go;
The feeling I lack has got me so.

TO MEMORIES

There's sadness in my heart and a tear within;
Perhaps it's goodbye, this is where it begins.

And so, you begin to accept the change,
For life is hard, it's never the same.
With your head up high and eyes ahead,
You look for the future; what lies ahead?
With the courage and grace of man,
You'll make it back; I know you can.
From where we've come, the child within,
And so, our journey from where it begins.
Upon each new step, so many we'll take;
We never look back, we'll never forsake.
And with new direction upon a new path,
A brighter future, a promise we'll be back.
And from the dawn, we build new hope,
And as for today, somehow we'll cope.
As for the future, it has its ways;
A new beginning, as a brighter day.
Perhaps as time, when things get tight,
Like falling apart, a change in mid-flight.
And with the seeds so begins the change,
And in the garden, the soul regains.
Upon a flower, grows big and strong,
And with the love, the caring belongs.
Each day you'll learn and strive for more;
You can endure; that's what love is for.
For all your values, it's more than friends,
For as our time, indeed, they'll lend.

And as the days, you'll learn and grow,
And deep inside, the memories will flow.
And with these friends and every goodbye;
For as the moments, we say we'll try.
Dear friends of mine, and for your thoughts,
A few I've added, the moment has brought.
For as the time, many days it'll be,
I'll hurry back, you wait and see.
Perhaps this day, it will be the last;
As the memories, they're forever in my grasp.
And with a smile and a sadness within,
So begins my task and the caring begins.

UPON THIS DAY OF SADNESS IN OUR HEARTS

In the silence, no voice do we hear,
No sounds of laughter, emptiness is feared;
No smile is found, no song in our hearts,
A loss in the family, one has embarked.
A journey for soul, one special man,
Fred gave to others, a helping hand.
A gentle man, whose hearts desired,
Fred reached new heights, in others he inspired.
We all knew it, we know he cared.
The love in his heart is something he shared.
Those who marvelled, life that he earned;
What time he shared, lessons we learned.
A father and brother, uncle and friend,
Inquisitive and spiritual, to the very end.
With prayer comes victory, strength comes will,
Patience comes virtue, in time comes skill.
Through cold and snow, wind and rain,
The rite of passage, Fred never complained.
Memories and faces, old places he'd been,
Photographs now cherished, something to be seen.
For family and friends, all who gathered near,
Remember his spirit, it still lingers here.

WITHOUT

How do I express what I am feeling inside?
Times I get scared, it's within that I hide.
Times I cannot speak, I lose the words,
Others seem lost and they don't deserve.

What is it; it's something inside?
How can I express what it is that hides?
Why am I afraid; what is it I know?
What to expect; how can I show?

Maybe in time, I will find a way,
To rid this thing, scares me away.
Is it just me; is the reason unknown?
Is it inside; have I always known?

I wait and wonder for a reason to be;
I am looking from within, wanting to see.
How can I find that which is my voice?
Where do I search; do I have a choice?

The voice that speaks, the one within,
The one that reasons, it's where it begins.
Maybe in thought and more to see,
Sit back and relax, find a way to be.

Now I wonder, what can I do?
How can I resolve and still be true?
I close my eyes and await to arrive,
One thing within that seems it's alive.

THE FINAL CHAPTER

Many faces have I seen,
Many places and still I dream.
Many years have passed me by,
Looking to heavens up to the sky.
Many faces I have met,
Many more I will forget.
A certain few I have come to know,
Cherished memories within I hold.
In many words I have expressed,
In other ways, what shall I expect?
Within my eyes my memory of life,
My will to succeed I motion to fight.
So many years and now it's time,
A last gasp for air, I have lost some time.
A message for those, for all who read,
For this, but one, enjoy, take heed.

THE SEARCHING BEGINS AGAIN

I was awake yet sleeping here all along,
Dwelling in the shadows, dreaming I belong.
I searched within to find the light,
A feeling trapped, a sensation I'd fight.

The light entered unto my soul,
This is where I was once whole.
The true me has resurfaced anew,
Shadows, the remnants, inside I grew.

To radiate of purity to heart and soul,
Perhaps one day to become whole.
But I will no longer be alone;
Inside of me, I have a home.

I feel every fiber of my being;
Keeps others from really seeing.
It's something I can never hide,
My gift of being and empathy guides.

Finding the answer in the unknown, despite,
Soul-searching through rhythms of life.
Shredded to decay to find a way,
In the nothingness comes my way.

CHAPTER 3
HOW IT HAPPENED

A SECOND AGO

For but a moment, a second of time;
Now it's gone, it's changed each time.
Another second is gone, another still;
It will not change; it has no will.
Upon each moment, it is so brief,
To another change you will see.
After you read all that, you see,
For it will change, believe you me.
Something you've learned, something thought,
Another side, a moment you have brought.
And seconds later, you will recall,
What you have learned, remembering it all.
And for your time, I thank you again,
For spending time, dear friend.
Till we meet again, another time perhaps,
See you will see for what you've grasped.

THE BOOK

*As for a smile,
That gains a mile,
For life that is our own.
The path we choose,
We cannot lose,
It's there, it's close to home.*

*As the night,
That guides the light,
The path that is our own.
When we speak,
Rewards we reap,
Our life within has grown.*

*To our friends,
They will lend,
The time that is our own.
In that we share,
To have and care,
The spirit is just on loan.*

*As the road,
With friends and foes,
For what we must overcome.
The obstacles we rise,
We learn to strive,
When we live and learn we've won.*

In our hands,
The words that stand,
The lines, the meaning will grow.
As the verse,
We learn these words,
The words that we will know.

We speak of truth,
The words that move,
The meaning that all will know.
The soul's within,
The love begins,
We live and love and grow.

WALLED IN

For all around, there is a cage;
The walls that hold, control the rage.
The roof above, the floor below;
In this room the lives they hold.

No windows to see, no world around;
No space to view, so little sound.
No one to speak, without a friend;
No one to see, no ear to lend.

With cameras they view, to see just one;
Through realities lost, an insignificant one.
To watch and wait, to look and stare;
To see what's up; do they really care?

ENVIRONMENTALLY SOUND; JUST A BUBBLE

I wish to see that place out there,
The one I cannot see;
I wish someday that I can fly,
To spread my wings so free;
I wish that some would not stare,
This life I am alone;
I wish for freedom and a place to play,
My will inside has grown;
I wish to breathe the air so fresh,
And the wind upon my face;
I wish to smell a sweet, sweet rose,
And leave this desolate place;
I wish to run upon a field,
And roll upon the hay;
I wish to sneeze and know a cold,
I wish this every day;
I wish a friend that I can touch,
For one I hope to see;
I wish my time it too is short,
My life it will cease to be;
I wish this bubble it soon will go,
For I may never be;
I wish the air in that I breathe,
Someway I can be freed;
I wish this wish for all that know,
That someday will be;
I wish for time that it's so short,
My will may break, you'll see.

THE WALLS OF TIME

Long before the beginning of time,
The lakes that grew, the land that shined.
Upon the land so still and free,
Then an idea that changed history.
Grain elevators were built, a way of trade,
Plying through the lakes and making a wage.
Giants, they stood high upon the land,
Technology soon changed; few still stand.
Peaceful and silence, emptiness belonged,
Time had changed, progress dawned.
The lakes were born and ways of trade;
Life in these towns grew, years it stayed.
For man has made and taken away;
His use perhaps lies destined to fate.
Through bits of concrete, the bond has changed;
The haunting structure is not the same.
Once rising so high from the lake below,
The town that grew the waters that flowed.
A way of life, a means by the sea,
Now tattered and torn yet destined to be.
Through one window, the broken glass,
A picture window whose time has passed.
A door leads a way upon once stairs;
The path is gone, now emptiness is there.
Above the lakes, this place they came;
Many had been drawn, now it's changed.
Within the past, a history is gone;
A part of the heritage has since moved on.
A hulking mass, now broken and worn;

The soul is broken and taken away.
Yet silent it sits, the soul has moved on;
The freighters lie silent, where stillness belongs.
The passage of time now fades away;
The ships once shined, fewer pass this way.
Soon they'll be gone, just in time,
Remembering when, a memory of mine.
With these people, the years will pass;
Within their lives, a moment was grasped.
In the silence, the land is freed;
A meaning in time for all eternity.

THE BIG BANG

Simcoe grain elevators stood many years,
Ships plying the waters lessened every year.
A moment had come as many years remained,
The time has come, its usefulness changed.

Upon the thousands who braved the cold,
Who watched and waited this moment to show?
The day was cold, we were chilled to the bone,
These strong souls, our spirits they'd shown.

Upon the cold, the wind that chilled,
These souls took heart, a glimpse for a thrill.
The sun was bright, the bay gripped in ice,
Two feet thick, many hours we'd suffice.

The name of these locals, those we recall,
Weekends we played; we've surpassed them all.
In order of rank, in order of praise,
In order we strive, we've matched many days.

No match for the cold masked in many ways,
One who's always there, she's Auntie Denise McRae.
Another of the clan, a cousin in many respects,
A local of the town, she's Susie Musselman no less.

Now the leader many years it's been said,
The one who's been apart, Mr. Goddard, Uncle Fred.
The last of the clan, the writer of verse,
He's captain, chief Chris Goddard, well deserved.

Perhaps the cold, the winds that blew!
A gathering of family whose perseverance grew.
The time was here, the moment at last,
With seconds to spare, a bang and crash.

Then there was dust, the pictures were few;
We dashed to the car, where the warmth we knew.
Seemed hours we braved the cold to the heart;
Upon thousands we saw a future, we were a part.

WHEN THE GRAIN ELEVATOR FELL / THE TROOP AND THE TOWER

The grain elevator, a part of the town,
No longer needed, demolition was found.
The blast was heard for miles around,
Dead of winter, thousands gathered 'round.

Upon the darkness to strike with life,
The troop proceeds, so began the fight.
Piece by piece, the wall comes down,
Upon once life for a village, a town.

A maze of wires, windows, and stairs,
Whose winding ways a purpose to bare.
Tiny soul whose graceful course,
Tear at the giant with hulking force.

Upon each brick, the walls descend,
Each passing day a lifestyle ends.
With tools they try to break its will,
Each new day they are closer still.

With many whose will it took to build,
Now many more destroy the will.
Upon each blow, another brick falls,
With each new piece, a change for all.

ELEVATED TO THE EDGE

With tools they build, yet tiny and small,
Towering so high, dwarfed by it all.
Upon the roof, this structure stands,
Strong yet bold, resting in their hands.

Toppled yet weak, now dangling a spell,
Through force of man, the structure fell.
They break with force upon each day,
Teetering on the edge, this structure lays.

Its weight and force within many hands,
Its conquering force, so little that stands.
Soon it will be gone, the force of it all;
Soon nothing is left, just remembering it all.

A PATH THAT LEADS A WAY

The gate is always open,
The path that leads a way.
The wind now falls silent,
Sounds of voices are here today.

Patter of small footsteps,
Laughter is in the air.
Sounds of singing carolers,
Christmas makes festive flare.

Over the way they come,
Bringing cheer to a couple's heart.
Many years these souls relate,
The joyous humour remain a part.

For many years, the custom stood,
Many more hearts were warmed.
And for all a festive spirit,
Traditions of family whose time was born.

The passage of time changed;
Over the years few stopped by.
With families of their own,
The journey north, long goodbyes.

Now fallen trees block the way,
Snow drifts in familiar tracks.
Footsteps no longer guide the way;
Now it seems there is no way back.

Within the forest, beyond the trees,
The leaves are green, the river flows.
Just over the ridge, a creek believe,
A sea of scenes, the forest grows.

For once a path, a road once made,
Ideas engraved where dreams soared.
Where imagination acts, destinies played,
Where peacefulness stayed, legends are stored.

FOR THE MOMENT, THEN THERE WAS DUST

A time perhaps,
For little had lapsed,
Nothing shall enter the mind.
Free of thought,
Emptiness has brought,
Tranquility and peace take the mind.

Silence perhaps,
The moment to grasp,
The will being one, nothing is said.
To ponder aloud,
Expressions to shroud,
Thought empty from the head.

It fills the mind,
Seconds within time,
Listen, to the silence aloud.
A moment at peace,
All thoughts cease,
Expressions of voice without sound.

NO WILL OR RIGHT

Few who care,
Nor made aware,
Waste they wish to pitch.
Places they use,
Lands they abuse,
The roadside a gully or ditch.

Places to throw,
In numbers they go,
Convenience is a way of life.
To rid with ease,
There are souls to please,
Misuse is to kill a life.

No will or right,
No conscience to fight,
They do as they please.
The reasons unknown,
Times they have thrown,
Destruction to a land at peace.

Into the ditch,
Frequently pitched,
Unseen and out of the way.
A risk to take,
Caught they forsake,
A hefty fine will be paid.

A view not seen,
No care or means,
A hole in which to dispose.
The land not theirs,
Others who cared,
Garbage thoughts never arose.

Far from home,
Driving alone,
Cigarette butts they seem to fly.
Thousands are found,
Littering the ground,
Is there a reason why?

THIS TOO SHALL PASS

There is a feeling of uneasiness stored inside;
Its fragrance and scent should be analyzed.
Not often shared, this sensation within;
The body, the internal enzymes, begin.

The bacterium in the colon breaks down food;
Many types we ingest as a growing brood.
Endogenous gas of hydrogen and methane,
Inhalations of air, a cause some who blame.

The internal workings of the digestive tract;
The food goes in then the evil attacks.
Whether it's beans, broccoli, milk, or beer,
The odorous fragrance it presents here.

Cutting the cheese or breaking wind;
Breaking the silence, a giggle begins.
Pumping, trumping, tooting within;
The sound of a fart, a foul odour begins.

Fifteen times a day, this habit partakes,
For nothing can be done to have and forsake.
Notions and potions and pills galore,
Nothing can curb this flatulence stored.

As we age, in our digestive tract,
Breaking down food, less enzymes we attract.
Who is to blame, the culprit goes still?
Though none are ashamed, having no will.

Another day as our lives go forth;
Now remember all this silent force.
One day we will share a moment at last;
A special time and this too shall pass.

CHAPTER 4
IMAGINATION

BUT A PIECE OF PAPER, A THOUGHT

Tossed aside, but of no means,
A piece of time, a useless dream.
Hands so bold, strong yet weak,
Strength of one, another will seek.
Into the hands, a thought to write,
A chance of dream, a time despite.
Thrown away, a time of haste,
A piece, perhaps, what a waste.
Thoughts and dreams, a time of hope,
A second glance, a means to cope.
The ink will fade, the message blurred,
A time, perhaps, an expression of words.
Time will pause, without one word,
Meaning, thoughts, this time deserves.

BUT A FLICKER OF LIGHT

Hidden from sight, but a flicker of light,
Darkness seemed to surround,
Times, few have known emptiness, yet alone,
For not a soul is around.

A light appears, at times almost near,
Times it wards all away,
Moments it hides, suddenly, a surprise,
Taking the darkness away.

Warmth brought the light, fend off the night,
Changes to all who are aware,
Its beauty beheld wonders, casts a spell,
As darkness it looms out there.

Winds that blow fend off the cold,
Winds have silenced the light,
The warmth now fades, lights taken away,
Darkness again is bright.

LETTERS OF TIME

All I can see,
Being a part of me.
Choice, I have made,
Direction to wage.
Effort is mine,
Further place in time.
Gathering of words,
Hardest to verse.
Ideas brought to life,
Joy in which to write,
Knowledge that I know,
Lines that seem to flow.
Mind is reason to learn,
Now ability to discern.
Opportunity in which to read,
People who take heed.
Question it's all there,
Rare ideas to share.
Scenes and places everywhere,
Trails the ability out there.
Us searching still unknown,
Void a place far from home.
Words we seem to find,
X exact work in mind.
Youth sharing something new,
Zoo in which to follow through.

From A to Z,
Lessons to heed.
For all to see,
We all must read.

ME AND MY SHADOW

As I stand alone, not far from home,
The sun is always near.
Every step I take and try to escape,
But it follows me here.

The further I go, it follows me so,
How can I leave it behind?
I close my eyes and try to hide,
I see it every time.

I tried running away every day,
But it never leaves me alone.
I hid in the trees, covered by leaves,
There I was, I am not alone.

I went on the swing and tried everything,
Even jumped into the pool.
I went on the slide, hard as I tried,
It followed me to school.

I went in my home to be alone,
There it was behind me.
It's attached to my feet and won't let me be,
When can I be free?

I talked to the sun, I tried everyone,
I even told my aunt May.
She had some advice, just look twice,
Wait for a rainy day.

The next day, the sun went away,
I ran outside to see.
I looked at the ground, what I had found,
I lost my shadow, I'm free!

MIND GAMES

Does wonder, the mind, a change of time,
Suddenly not there.
Void of life, a loss of fight,
Unknowing one is aware.

Loss of thought, the mind forgot,
How it used to be.
Seemingly changed, life's rearranged,
Unable a chance to see.

A loss to feel, emotions not real,
An emptiness within time.
A moment alone, no place, no home,
Unknowingly this life is mine.

A darkened space, life's embrace,
My being, it's there.
No voice, no sounds, no beings around,
Thoughts within my feelings are aware.

Dull is the pain, emptiness changed,
To forget to feel again.
Changes within, where to begin,
Feelings unknowingly remain.

A loss of life, loss despite,
A void left a hole.
Changes in time, loss within mind,
Loss of life took a hold.

*A voice begins, a soul within,
Silence tells a tale.
Unfamiliar change, emotions sustained,
Life one does fail.*

RHYMES

For what is a rhyme, words set in time
Words within a verse, the next does deserve,
A story to tell, a new word to spell,
An idea to express, a word that's next,
An emotion to reveal, a broken heart to heal.

This is a test, do your best,
Find a simple word to rhyme,
Ideas were brought, some were not,
A story, a verse in time.

Now, remember when, the word at the end,
The word must be in rhyme.
Simple at best, what comes next,
An idea, a thought within time.

Simple is best, difficulty regrets,
Some words won't work, you'll see.
Words that are small, little letters, that's all,
Easier, yet simple, you'll agree.

The rules may change,
Words stay the same.
The verse is short,
Good luck, sport.

Time now flies,
For I must go,
Remember now,
Words should flow.

*The alphabet works,
If you know how to spell,
Ask a teacher, she'll help,
Goodluck, goodbye, and farewell.*

TEACHING A LESSON LEARNED AND SAVOURED AGAIN

Perhaps a time that comes to mind,
A challenge we all must face.
A chance to relate and take a break,
A moment none can replace.

The early years, a challenge not feared,
Eager to prove to all.
What tasks at hand, we plundered and planned?
The respect we seek above all.

Many hours we slaved, long nights we stayed,
To prove we had the knack.
A loss of sleep, all night we seek,
To understand and never look back.

Quizzes and questions and daunting reflections,
Through pages too numerous to count.
Each question savoured, understanding and behaviour,
Attendance and each name in which to pronounce.

The dawn of the day, we hope and pray,
The challenge, the ability to reach.
A spare to partake, a moment to forsake,
For today all students will behave.

TIMELESS SIMPLE TRUTH

A flower,
But once a seed,
But a drop of rain,
In the soil it's freed.

A pond,
But drops of rain,
To drink in life,
Through life sustained.

Life,
It will not die,
A soul of one,
To live and thrive.

Sun,
Warmth abounds,
The cover of life,
Through endless surrounds.

Rock,
Unto a pond,
Ripples away,
Life moves on.

Tree,
Seeds once sewn,
Life is freed,
Forever its grown.

TO TOUCH THE SKY

Since man could think and see,
He has looked and wondered,
And longed to touch the sky.

Since man has learned to dream,
He has wished to steal a star,
And reached to touch the moon.

Since man has learned to build,
He has built temples to the heavens,
And reached for immortality above.

Since man has learned to fly,
He has seen the illusion of the sky,
And knows it is not there.

Since man has left this tiny world,
He has learned of what the stars are made,
And walked upon the moon.

Since man has learned to understand,
He has lost the mystery of life,
And forgotten how to dream.

A TOUCH OF GREEN

Tis the time of year,
Alas that we fear,
For we'd be jolly and green.
Let us share the wealth,
Share our good health,
Only now we'd be seen.
Leprechauns we are called,
A wee bit small,
Fast and flourish, we are proud.
If you don't mind,
Be gracious and kind,
For this day we are a wee bit loud.
Yet above all,
If you must call,
To be seen, we must be heard.
Upon this day,
We'll enlighten our way,
For green is not absurd.
A moment of your time,
A moment you won't mind,
Tis green is what you wear.
Stand up and be proud,
Wear it out loud,
Show us that you really care.
Perhaps you will share,
Have and take care,
For this is but one day.
Now raise your glass,
For green you will grasp,

For green you shall look today.
When you call to mind,
These words at this time,
They must be whispered out loud.
Don't raise your voice,
For you have a choice,
Remember, wear green and be proud.
For it is green, that is green,
It's only green, that is green,
Only green is green when it is green.
Green when it's green,
It's green only green,
Green when is green it's been.

CHAPTER 5
OBSERVATIONS

AN IDEA?

As in the silence, the time draws near,
Within an idea, that's thoughts revered;
As for the patience, the times allowed,
Collects one's thoughts, together somehow;
With a means to think, a way to voice,
To find that meaning, the words of choice;
Yet so many words from which to choose,
To find the ones yet not confuse;
A path is taken, the road is clear,
Through these words, idea draws near;
As for the words, each falls into place,
Describing what is in a mannered state;
The meanings now chosen, the stories said,
An idea now taken, for now it's read;
As time moves on, each thought appears,
The final verse, the end is near;
At last, the line, these words are found,
The poem is clear, the meanings abound.

TO PICTURE TO PLACE TO RELATE

Wise is the master,
Brave is the mate,
Cunning is the hero,
Strong wins the race.
Understanding the knowledge,
Reading will sustain,
Reasoning is the cause,
Will to survive remains.
Idea is a thought,
Write will imprint,
Memory will not lose,
Recall in an instant.
Object with a meaning,
Hands in which to work,
Knowledge with to reason,
Vision it will work.
Determined is a thought,
Motivated is the one,
Outcome is the reason,
One shared with one.

AFTER THE COLD

No longer does the wind blow cold,
Or the snow that seems to fall.
No longer is there a grip of pain,
The numbing feeling is nothing at all.

No longer does the temperature rise,
Or the warmth enters our souls.
No longer does the cold affect us,
This feeling we do not even know.

No longer do we rise to the warmth,
For zero does not exist.
No longer do we look for the weather,
The cold just seems to persist.

The wind that blows a grip of pain,
Each layer the temperature drops.
The hats, scarves, gloves, and more,
We get to zero, the temperature doesn't stop.

It's so cold, reality seems lost,
Sensations of warmth, feeling is not.
Upon the layers of clothes persist,
Though moving, takes a bit.

BIRDS OF FLIGHT

*Perhaps a crowd now gathers there,
A time of better, of friends who care.
For the moment, there is no sound,
No echoes of voice, no movements found.*

*Within the team, the spirit flows,
Within to each, a friendship grows.
Upon the voices, in each there's one,
But as together, this moment becomes.*

*Upon the board, yet round and old,
Within the strings of silver and gold.
The birds of flight upon their wings,
These flightless birds, in the air they sing.*

*It's in the weight, the shaft and length,
It's lift and flight, a test of strength.
Within a flair, its chosen scheme,
Its feathers stiff, its colours gleam.*

*In the hand, the eye now reads,
Upon the board, the arrow takes heed.
Then the throw, through the air,
It's cast with ease, its target there.*

*Within the throw, the arm and wrist,
With skill and speed, the points persist.
With each new throw, patience, and speed,
Only in time, the confidence will heed.*

With a smile upon the face,
With this feeling can never replace.
Upon each throw, the guidance and ease,
The dart performs with grace and speed.

A loft in the air, accurate and precise,
The targets chosen; the outcome sufficed.
Upon the days, through skill and time,
Then a feeling, the moment will shine.

A special few, whose patience succeed,
Will reap the benefits, the reward is believed.
In the best, the points shall rise,
Within the team and before your eyes.

In the days to come, a sense of pride,
Because you've earned, because you tried.

BELIEF

Strong is the face,
Courageous is the man,
Humble is his beginning,
Forever does he stand.
Within the war,
There is a soul,
The one who rules,
The one who controls.
Few friends he makes,
Short-lived are they,
Their will to fight,
Short is their stay.
For there he stands,
He's the only one left,
All others have gone,
Is he to be next?
A tear within his eyes,
For he must stand,
He will not cry,
For he's a man.

GARBAGE TO END OF THE WASTE

Looks can be deceiving,
The ones who are receiving,
The many who must do.
For some have the job,
Of disposing the blob,
The job is revolting, that's true.
The longer it sits,
It soon makes us sick,
It attracts all the flies.
Try as we may,
To get out of the way,
It begins to water our eyes.
Different sizes and shapes,
It's hard to escape,
And always in the way.
It's always there,
It's hard to bear,
We can never get away.
A place of their own,
A place called home,
A space too disgusting for us all.
Not to mention the smell,
On hot days it dwells,
The flies seem to have a ball.
It becomes a chore,
There's always more,
More time that we spend.
They haul it away,
Any form, any way,

Where will it all end?
It becomes a pest,
Like all the rest,
We try to find a way.
Wherever we go,
There's always a flow,
I guess it's here to stay.
There is no room,
Soon we'll be doomed,
There's no place we can go.
We're running out of land,
No place we can stand,
Where are we supposed to go?

HOW CAN I HELP?

How often it's heard, the sound of the word,
At times that we need it the most.
It is a chance, a moment, a glance,
The word gives us hope!
A calming voice, the one by choice,
Just one who can come through.
An idea, a thought, this feeling has brought,
To a friend who is truly you.
A helping hand, one with a plan,
The ability to put in place.
A simple gesture, more than a pleasure,
See the act face to face.
The courage of one, is more than some,
A feeling of being apart.
Warmth now shared, knowing you cared,
The love found in your heart.
Reach out and touch, resonates so much,
Knowing in an expression of hope.
Within one heart, a calming part,
To the ones who need it the most.
Do a chore, run to the store,
Write a letter, call on the phone.
A simple pleasure, a moment to treasure,
You are not in this alone.
Call on a friend, some time to spend,
Let them know that you care.
Help with a task or just ask,
It's knowing they are now aware.
A feeling of hope, your ability to cope,

*With all that is around you somehow.
Dealing with change, life is rearranged,
How can I help you, now?*

IT'S GOOD

A word often heard,
Does it deserve,
What it is that's good?
Is it what's said,
Or what's dread?
What is being, it's good.

What is wrong,
Does it belong,
What is it that's missing?
What to expect,
What is next,
What is it that thing?

Those who hear,
A sense of fear,
To each is something changed.
What it lacks,
What attracts,
The answer is expected to change.

It's not a word,
But what's heard,
It's not the question why.
A sense of change,
A means of shame,
Reality is still wondering why.

Lost in thought,
It hasn't brought,
The feeling it's supposed to fulfil.
The emotions inside,
The ability tried,
The response, the space hasn't filled.

A smiling face,
A loss of place,
The voice now what's heard.
A loss to try,
To reason why,
A means, a loss of the word.

Perhaps the word,
Does not deserve,
And less it should be used.
It doesn't agree,
It will not heed,
The response is often abused.

KNOWING THE THOUGHT PROCESS

Words not said, feelings expressed,
It's knowing inside just what to expect.
Ways of understanding something known,
Times of observing, not always shown.

A process of thought, something revealed,
Sayings and not feelings concealed.
Dealings within just the right words,
Where to begin so not to disturb.

Ways to recall motion in time,
To consider them all, so sets the rhyme.
As ideas abound, questions concealed,
Feelings surround, answers revealed.

Though writing begins, ideas revolve,
Ideas sink in, the true meanings evolve.
So set in time, the meanings thrive,
So begins the rhyme, ideas arrive.

Short gestures of time, pen will write,
Words and verses soon take flight.
Before long the job is almost done,
The time seems long for everyone.

RHYMES AND REASONS, WORDS OF THOUGHT

A means to make you laugh,
Bring a smile to your face,
Bring a tear to your eye,
Leaving a lasting embrace.

To take you away,
Down in depth of man,
Explore new places,
To let you understand.

Leave you with a thought,
A question to ask,
An idea to wonder,
A piece of the past.

Take you beyond the stars,
To a world unknown to us,
To embrace a child,
The family in all of us.

With the far reaches of time,
Thousands of feet below,
New place, not yet found,
Meet someone you don't know.

Teach you about love,
Take you away from death,
Hear the sounds in the forest,
Wonder what's coming up next.

Listen to the sounds of nature,
Wonder about the rain,
Look up to the sky,
Why is it we feel pain?

Look inside ourselves,
To see what we are,
Look upon our world,
To reach to the stars.

SMOKE GETS IN YOUR EYES

Though it offends,
Those with friends,
All who are around.
It hangs in the air,
It doesn't seem fair,
Lingering without a sound.

Sweet smelling it may be,
It's very hard to see,
It clouds up the room.
Its unique odour,
Milder at times bolder,
Killing all the fresh air fumes.

Confined to one room,
With life-threatening fumes,
There's no place to go.
As the day goes on,
It's potentially strong,
It's having no place to go.

It gets in our clothes,
Offending the nose,
The smell, it won't go away.
Until you leave,
Try to reprieve,
Try washing it away.

It burns the eyes,
Pain, you want to hide,
Satisfaction, you just can't part.
It's always in the air,
You try to grin and bare,
Quitting seems so hard to part.

Signs hang in the air,
Reminding all to be aware,
Smoking is not allowed.
But it still goes on,
Every day and beyond,
It still goes unnoticed somehow.

THE GREAT SHELVING DEBATES

A moment has passed, a moment lapsed,
An idea that came to light,
Within a thought, this moment had brought,
A genius with creative insight.

To create and design, to develop over time,
To fashion into wood,
This shelf would display, hidden ideas to portray,
Within the depths stood.

With tools in hand, Danny worked the plan,
A blueprint to his success,
A ruler to measure, to fashion a treasure,
Precise cuts would progress.

For wood will inspire, to develop a desire,
The mouldings soon take shape,
With a saw in hand, safety to the plan,
The shelf will begin to take shape.

With drill in hand, the depth you've planned,
A hole within to screw,
To cut and glue, to see his way though,
Nailed it and fastened too.

Now hinged in place, within the space,
Seamlessly within Danny's design,
With locks disguised, the magnets will rise,
The shelf and secret you may find.

THE GOLF BALL DIVING CHAMPIONSHIP, A STORY INSPIRED

Strategical placed from a club and a tee,
Its flight and trajectory one might see.
There are some who say it's a daunting task;
Search a murky bottom, a token to grasp.
Yet hidden beneath a treasure to hold;
It's white in shape yet round as gold.
A shiny object that's round yet smooth;
To hold on tight, you cannot lose.
A shiny object that's hidden from sight;
To search and scour, to hold on tight.
Beneath the rocks and boulders disguise,
Just hidden underneath the spherical hides.
With goggle and mask, a vision too see,
Yet crisp and clear, the outcome will be.
The task at hand, with time to spare,
To seek the reward for all to share.
A gasp of air to dive into the deep,
Where rocks are hidden, crayfish creep.
To swim so long so precious of life;
To hold one's breath, a token in sight.
Up to the surface, a gasp to the air;
A breath of life, a prize to share.
A bag is chosen for the treasure hold;
Counting each ball and closer to the goal.
To catch one's breath and dive down again;
Exhaustions and excitement may never end.
A look of surprise and a happy laugh;
Now treading water and still going back.

A day of fun and another surprise;
Capturing the trophy, a feeling inside.
Tomorrow, the task to drive with pride;
Now, the bounty of riches and another try.
The balls of summer, just let them fly;
The days of summer, you cherish inside.

THE DAILY GRIND

Some might say, one challenge per day,
The cost for a coffee, you'll agree.
For those who are assured, we hold to our word,
Proof is the passion, you'll believe.

Some words of choice, echoes in our voice,
For coffee is not what it seems.
Many new flavours, one must savour;
It's not just another coffee bean!

The Flavia flavours they ask, creations will surpass;
The concoction we all will create.
Cookies to savour, many sorted flavours,
To sweeten or powder, to lighten or debate.

A Splenda Choice, Equal to voice,
Sugar Twin or just one cube.
To cream or milk, powdered skim and lactose,
A challenge all will review.

Foam cups and paper, the flavour to savour;
The senses are all but aroused.
The brewing, the taste, one minute, no haste;
It's all the time has allowed.

With Starbucks and K-Cups, Timothy's, and teas,
Of Tazo, Bigelow, and Lipton.
In bags or beans, in packs with seams;
Temptation, one must give in.

Upon the plates, where spoons debate,
Forks and knives may fold.
Where filters will screen impurities between,
And stream out the old.

Cleaning perhaps an arduous task;
Rubber gloves, this choice is made.
Cascade with foil, Squeak'n Clean will toil;
Coffee grounds will just vanish away.

J Cloths, a dream, papers towels to clean,
Sunlight to lighten the way.
With detergent fresh cups, and Palmolive plus,
In garbage bags, they're just thrown away.

TIME FLIES

We live in a world that is,
Not in a world that should be.
We accept the things we cannot change,
Courage to change the things we can,
The wisdom to know the difference.

We must take the time to think,
   It's the source of power.
Take the time to play,
   It's the secret to perpetual youth.
Take time to pray,
   It's the greatest power on the earth.
Take time to read,
   It's the foundation of wisdom.
Take time to be friendly,
   It's the road to happiness.
Take time to laugh,
   It's the magic of the soul.
Take time to give,
   It's too short a day to be selfish.

YES, IT'S MONDAY MORNING AGAIN!

As for the moment, the time is delayed;
It's really morning, is it today?
As for the weekend, where has it gone?
It's Monday already; it must be wrong!

As for the alarm, echoing those sounds,
Deep within sleep, where silence abounds.
As for the hours, the clock is wrong;
I cannot be late; I didn't sleep long.

The minutes, the time, it's late;
No time to hesitate; shit! I'm late.
A thought, perhaps, a moment or two;
Time to reflect, with perspective, view.

To place a call, to tell them I am late;
Now, in a hurry, I cannot debate.
The thought, it's mine, and mine alone,
A thoughtful gesture, I thought I'd phone.

I dial the number, for it's all a blur;
What do I say, what are the words?
The connection goes through, I wait for a sign,
I wait for the answer; it's a long time.

It rings and rings and rings some more,
It rings so loud, what are they waiting for?
It seems like forever, yet no one's there,
I tried my best; I guess they don't care.

I count the rings, just a hundred or so;
With all those people, what's a secretary for?
As the time, it's way past now;
I grab my stuff and wonder somehow.

As for the time, it's Monday, oh well;
The day is beginning, as I can tell.
Perhaps a wish, just this one,
For the day to end, just a short one.

I jump into the car and down the road;
I hit the Tim Hortons, hot cup of Joe.
Yes, I forgot, it's Monday again;
I am retired; it's back to bed again.

WORTHWHILE

It's easy enough to be pleasant,
When life flows like a song.
The one worthwhile is the one who will smile,
When everything goes dead wrong.

For the test of the heart is trouble,
It always comes with years.
The smile that is worth the praise of the earth,
Is the smile that shines through tears.

It's easy enough to be prudent,
When nothing tempts you to stray.
When without or within, no voice or sin,
Is luring your soul away.

But it's only a negative virtue,
Until it is tried by fire.
Life that is worth the honour of our earth,
Is the one that raises desire.

With virtue, the son, and the father,
Who has no strength for the strife.
The world's highways are combined today;
They make up the sum of life.

The virtue that conquers passion,
The sorrow that hides the smile;
It is these that are worth the homage,
We find them but once in a while.

CHAPTER 6
POINT OF VIEW

BEYOND THE FOREST

In the forest lies thousands of trees,
There is a path that's scattered by leaves.
Up the hill and around the bend,
The path that leads seems to never end.
Up the rise and down the hill,
The old growth trees, grow there still.
By the creek, the river that flows,
And guards the way for few still know.
As the trees that crowd the light,
The sun that shines, canopy below to night.
In the forest now, hidden away,
There stands a cabin for many a day.
Upon the path, broken yet worn,
That the creek has flooded and scorn.
There is a gate that leads the way,
Fence twisted, rusted, still blocking the way.
Now it's open, the gate still ajar,
The way is clear and vacant by far.
As the trail, still lined with stones,
The vines and weeds now lie here overgrown.
Once footsteps travelled this way,
Now, in stillness, nature guards it today.

FAR HORIZON

A place so far, I have never seen,
So few but some have ever been.
I look to search, but hope to find,
The answer within the truth, the rhyme.
Today, the story for now unfolds;
Search for truth, the mystery withholds.
I look and stare but cannot see,
For in this space, it cannot be.
I see within my eyes to sight,
The magic within, my will to fight.
My only hope, the will to try,
Across the horizon, within the sky.
To light my way, to search within,
This is where my search begins.

KEEPERS OF THE NIGHT

In the distance, so dark and cold,
With warmth within, for few will know.
No sign of light, no direction to aid,
The mariners found this desolate place.
A passage through waters, a challenge to some,
A loss to vessels, to navigate and overcome.
Within the darkness, a compass to aid,
A prayer to God, many lives to save.
In winter storms and blinding rain,
Through dark of night, they remained.
The mariners' task, to deliver supplies,
An arduous task, some realized.
For many years, the loss of lives,
The lucky ones remained alive.
For those whose voice was never heard,
A loss so great an answer deserved.
Limestone towers, the imperial kind,
Rose like trees, one at a time.
As the nights, the light soon arose,
Lightening the shoals, navigation aid rose.
Dark and desolate was this place,
Miles from home, a light keeper's space.
Within the light, the warmth is around,
Circling the bay, the lighthouse is found.
Atop the tower, the light appears,
The light within, the power is here.
Upon the rock, the island dwells,
A lonely life, the light keeper's spell.
Through dark of night, the winds that blows,

Into the hearts of the sailors who know.
Through the channel and narrow straits,
The rocks and shoals are a mariner's fate.
Just beneath the rocky shoal, water stirs,
In wrecks and rubble, the bay preserves.
Ships of sail, steam, propeller, and steel,
Crushed with force below are concealed.

THE LIGHT WITHIN

Perhaps for one there's something more,
As the time it's worth searching for.
As the souls that's found inside,
The will and truth, they search to try.
As the soul, the spirit that shows,
The feeling within, the light grows.
As the warmth, the feeling resides,
For the knowledge is soon realized.
As each one, the will to strive,
As the journey, to search, souls alive.
And as the road, the way is clear,
Just one, the voice is near.
In that time, the warmth abounds,
This feeling inside, the warmth surrounds.
For the truth, for it's now aware,
The light has come, the feelings there.

SO, FEW HAVE KNOWN

I look to find and hope to see,
The river of light, the light in me,
To journey away, one will find,
The meaning of life, truth behind,
Time it seems, time has lapsed.
Who takes a hold, a thought to grasp?
Wonders within, a place, one thought,
The memories whose time has forgot,
A place so few have ever dreamed,
So few but some have ever been,
This place though none can forsake,
This is a time, a place for keepsakes.

THROUGH CHANGES

Here lies a house once lived in, now broken and old, worn by the sun and rain.
Within the voice the sounds echo of laughter, distant sounds of children long ago.
The walls of time as kids who once played, crayon drawings faded on the walls.
The pictures reveal a deepened desire, a truth whose meaning has yet to be discovered.
Old picture, the frames now gone, the sun streams in, just a faded outline remains.
If the walls could speak, the sounds of laughter echo the joy and celebration of life.
Whose soul has yet to be shared, the feelings thirst for the longing some time ago.
A child who finds their mystical and magical place in life, imagination embellishes a meaning.
Whose dreams, as the key to life itself, whose inner peace wills one to continue.
The curtain now tattered and torn wallpaper now peeling, the wood floor worn down by footsteps.
Thoughts and ideas, the memories dance like flames of a candle in the wind, cascades alongside.
Where smiles, fond memories, bring joy and desire, as in time the days begun have now gone.
Where the words and understanding of writing is lost in the verse to a feeling of existence.
Where the light ceases to be, death changes the outlook on life, yet the limitless void.
As our existence, as time embellishes our sense of true being.

THE CAPTAIN

*Nothing does he fear,
White hair, grey beard,
For age has changed his face.
So strong and bold,
His training took hold,
Wisdom and learned in place.*

*So wise and true,
Making his mark, he knew,
Strong men he would need.
He held on tight,
Death to fight,
Losing, he would not heed.*

*Honesty and greed,
Would make him heed,
His spirit is all he had.
Through storms and gales,
He set his sails,
Journey though good and bad.*

*He would head north,
Setting sails, a driving force,
Within his spirit would take hold.
Strong was his pride,
The fear he'd hide,
The course to navigate in his soul.*

The seas were rough,
He's never given up,
Knowledge and charts he could spare.
With courage and skill,
An unfaltering will,
At times he was not aware.

Few friends or foes,
Faces he's not known,
Lighthouses, landmarks he had seen.
His will to fight,
To keep the right,
Sailing was all he had dreamed.

The captain is gone,
Now retired and moved on,
In our eyes, he is still here.
Thought in a storm,
You'll hear the horn,
You'll know he's coming near.

Do not fear,
If you cannot hear,
The soul will bring to light.
The dreams he shares,
He always cares,
The will, the courage, to fight.

WHERE THE SPIRIT STILL LIES

To the best of 2022,
2021, a year all who tried.
A special thanks to each,
Just to stay healthy still applies.

A prayer to those of our friends,
The ones who have come and gone.
Memories, we keep them within,
In our hearts they now belong.

The season is now upon us,
For the feeling we all share.
For those so special to remember,
Many thanks in knowing you cared.

For now, the year will end,
A moment in all our lives.
To a happy and healthy new year,
For tomorrow our dream still lies.

Merry Christmas, my friends,
To all of us, indeed.
A hope we survive this one,
COVID free, we all agree.

To all our friends and family,
To each a sense of pride.
The moment of family is shared,
Where the spirit still lies.

THE WRITE STUFF

Many faces, and now I have seen,
Many places, and still I dream.
So much to do, I wish for time,
Perhaps the loss, and so it's mine.

The time to voice, I do still lack,
Express in words, the ability to back.
What I hear and not the word;
It's what I do, the expression in verse.

What I do to just get by;
It pays the bills, you ask why.
For many years, I struggle within,
Knowledge, I lack, your answer begins.

As I try, and to succeed,
Your voice I hear does not agree.
So put in words as now I say,
If not for me, be on your way.

In my words, I have the rights,
To put in rhymes some flow in flight.
Perhaps one day, my will to find,
The key to stratum, the key is mine.

To voice my words, to show to all,
This one is mine, I'll make the call.
For all who are here, the time is right,
So, I deserve, I have the rights.

CHAPTER 7
HISTORY

DARKENED PEACE, SOULS RELEASE

Listen to me, a story you will see,
A time long ago.
A stormy night, death would ignite,
A place some sailors will go.

The night had dawned, the ship sailed on,
Searching the darkness for a light.
The waves did rises unto the skies,
To find the shoreline in sight.

Winds blew strong, the ship struggled on,
Snow and rain changed in the night.
The biting cold soon took a hold,
One by one, sailors losing the fight.

All seems black and no way back,
Darkness comes from within.
No light had seen, no one had been,
Void of light would begin.

The end was near, to cease the fear,
Sailing a means, a way of life.
Into the light, the souls bright,
And into the peace, goodnight.

No soul would ease a voice to breathe,
As echoes in the night.
Silence befell to cast a spell,
Within the eyes are fright.

The blackened night and filled with fright,
A voice one did hear.
Though not afraid, a voice will say,
Come closer and see me near.

A voice cast out, a body did shout,
The soul's release has freed.
A light did shine, a soul did find,
Darkness of the night had ceased.

The soul at peace, the pain has ceased,
The light, the soul did find.
A way and a means, to find within dreams,
A moment, a piece of time.

As the day will pass, a time perhaps,
A voice will call beyond.
To tell a tale, some time to sail,
And the voice to carry on.

FORGOTTEN REMAINS DISCOVERED

Many feet below,
Lost in the darkened cold,
Away from the warmth of the sun's rays.
Another world reigns,
As new life sustains,
Though destined to be discovered one day.

Down through murky depth,
Far below, life has left,
Buried in the silt-covered ruins.
Where life casts no lights,
Cold surrounds a lifeless fight,
Undiscovered are lost ships, bottom strewn.

Once broken, silence survives,
Hundreds of years, sea life thrives,
For one glimpse of a time long past.
Time has silenced the sea,
Shattered frozen for all eternity,
One looks a journey one will grasp.

A world touched by another,
Disturbed remains now discovered,
Shattered remains fall to the sea.
A single life withstands,
Many of different lands,
Overgrown are these ships where life deceives.

KEEPER OF THE LIGHT, HOPE ISLAND

Through the warmth of the sun, leaves of green,
The waters are warmed in the summer scene.
In the days of old, the time now past,
These summers have gone, time has lapsed.

A place I knew some time ago,
A time of the past, the memories unfold,
The cool waters flowed, the seas of green,
Wonders as a lad, a place I still dream.

On the crest of the hill, the cliffs of rock,
Place of old, the lightkeepers walked.
Perched on the hill, a grove of trees,
Northern pines crowded over the seas.

Patches of grass rose like fire,
Thrashing like the seas ever higher.
Upon the house, for it is red,
Within the lights, the stories said.

In this place so different, so unique,
For here it sits, as passersby seek.
Within the lights, a glow of red,
Yet stored inside, a love now bred.

To gaze inside, a moment in time,
This love perhaps, carried though time.
Its shape unique, its height so tall,
The light surrounds, many have recalled.

For little shade would ever come,
Harsh was the land so few would succumb.
The keeper of the light, through history's told,
Harsh was the job, a destiny bestowed.

For in the light, the legends told,
The secret of the light, the mystery unfolds.
Though dark and desolate is this place,
The rocks below are marked with fate.

For many years or so it's been told,
The keeper of the light, this honour bestowed.
The measure of a man his duties to forsake,
Through understanding, knowledge, the job he makes.

The light from within is a different source,
Though destiny chooses its fateful course.
The secret of the journey, this way beholds,
Within the light, the journey unfolds.

Within the light that guards the source,
The waves below crush with force.
High above the cliffs of stone,
The light breaks a friendly form.

Keeper of the light, beware he warns,
The light that shines, its haunting form.
For many years, the lighthouse shined,
Light keeper job, a memory in time.

Time has passed, technology dawned,
The way of the light keeper is gone.
Harsh is the land, with wind and rain,
The house of light was never the same.

Through the night, the light did surround,
The island and shoal, the horn did sound.
A time did come, the house is gone,
Keeper of the light has since moved on.

LIFE REMNANTS REMAIN

Emptiness, silence, souls still roam;
Crushed remains of a forgotten home.
Once beaten path, leads to the door;
Lost are the faces, now no more.

The walls of stone now remain;
What little of life these walls sustained.
Lost are the voices once etched and more;
Cherished are the memories forever stored.

The steps below are barely still seen;
Overgrown are the weeds of green.
The cellar cold now leading below;
Once dark and damp, the root cellar grows.

From once the floor the cellar stored;
Preserved food in jar and more.
Jars and bottles broken remain;
Sealed some time ago, freshness sustained.

Buried beneath in the layers of time;
Remnants of life cherished in mind.
Hidden until now lost from sight;
Of a time once forgotten sustaining life.

For just beneath, a time gone by;
Through feet of rubble, reveal these signs.
Strange bottles and jars of a time gone by;
Unfamiliar are these shapes, remnants of a time.

No more are the signs of laughter;
No more do the voices cry out.
No more are the memories still held;
The fire is over, the silence is out.

THE LIGHTHOUSE

Towering above the waters so high,
Few windows are seen, dwarfed by its size.
All around the windows that shine,
Inside a light over a watchful eye.
Above the cliffs and rocks that hide,
The light is seen circling the sky.
Into the darkness, the light is seen,
Warning of the rocks, the shoals are not seen.
The shallow waters are hidden by waves,
As for the shoals that darken this way.
Passing ships that travel, so be aware,
The light that shines, have, and take care.
In the fog, the horn that sounds,
Shoals and reefs, the unsuspecting grounds.
The lighthouse's role, a captain's friend,
The light set aglow, warmth that lends.

OVER THE WAY ONCE, THE COW PATH LEADS

For many years or so it's been,
Many more few have ever seen.
A place we knew yet hidden within,
Few ventured where the path begins.
The space we knew sometime before,
Was hidden away with secrets galore.
For many years this place survived,
Until the past years, nature thrived.
The path that leads up the hill,
The secret trails, the legends still.
Up to the crest, silver birches grew,
Along the edge, an adventurous brood.
Following the trail to the end,
A gravel road upward to the bend.
Unto a gate, now left ajar,
Open for those who ventured this far.
Down the road and up the rise,
The view from here soon realized.
Wild apple trees lined the road,
Summer season, a bountiful load.
Down the road to the crest to view,
The land below and islands too.
Down the hill to venture away,
Perhaps to return another day.
Trails, hidden treasures once seen,
Has fallen to ruins, lost in my dreams.

Trees of old now hide the way,
Crowding the path that carried those days.
Memories of time, shared by all,
Few who travelled were cherished by all.

OVER THE WAY THEY CAME

Through broken pieces of rubble worn,
A path beaten and washed away by storms.
Over the way, they used to come,
Footsteps traced this way for some.

Through the forest they travelled on by,
Trees that huddled, crowding the sky.
Hand-laden stones, laid end to end,
Holding back the ground, a home to spend.

Weeds and trees have weaved away,
Blanketing the home that's here today.
Wooden rails once carved from a tree,
From on the path their way was freed.

Many years have come and gone,
The way of the forest has moved on.
The path covered over, no means to see,
Bushes and shrubs, as nature runs free.

Homestead stood where the stones once laid,
The fire is over, burned timbers remain.
Nature has changed what the home is today,
The forest has claimed yet another day.

POINT OF NO RETURN

Within the body, these cells abound,
Within one life, destiny surrounds.
There is a choice, just one to decide,
A moment for one soon realized.
Through facts and figures a decision's made,
The chance for one, a life to save.
Within many months, a chance to seek,
Control the virus, a cure to reap.
Each day, the hour, a moment for one,
The signs, a thought, to overcome.
For reason unknown, each one relives,
For family and friends, support that gives.
A deterrent to radiate, a struggle for one,
A treatment, one cure, and hope for some.
The emotions, the grind, each minute will pass,
Just one more day, the hope will last.
Through many changes, a life will lapse,
Unto the journey, this life has passed.

RIVER OF LIFE

Upon the stream that runs at ease,
Floating on the surface, coloured leaves.
The current that moves, winding its way,
Over rock and roots, hastening this way.
Down it flows, even faster it speeds,
Within, carrying life, for nature breathes.
Crystal clear in the waters so blue,
Buried beneath, new life shines through.
Within the pool, it slows the speed,
The light that shines, so begins the seed.
Through the window around new life,
The water delivers thirst-quenching life.

RUINS OF YESTERYEAR, GREAT SHIPS LIE BENEATH THE WATERS

In the chilling gloom of Georgian Bay,
For many years, they still lie here today.
Ships and remnants and forgotten past,
Moments to remember, a lifetime to grasp.

Through uncharted waters nature would play,
A struggle for those who hardened their ways.
As for the storms, few who survived,
The waters so cold, most men would die.

Few who have come to see still don't know,
Men who once lived for their stories now told.
Life was harsh, for the seas would tell,
Late autumn storms, more luck, less farewell.

For down below, resting just beneath,
The ships of sail, their last retreat.
In these ships, our history now stands,
Abandoned and deserted upon foreign lands.

CHRIS GODDARD "SILVERGHOST"

THE CHOSEN FEW

Perhaps for few, I have ever seen,
Perhaps less have ever been.
There are so few have yet to see,
Only reality has yet, only one can be.

And yet to see but only a glimpse,
A chance to be and less of sense.
Still a chance to grasp a part of life,
As time is short to live one life.

A way of life, a means to reason,
To see what is to believe in.
View through one's eyes, few have seen,
There is of life, the chosen have seen.

There is so much and yet to see,
The will of life and so to believe.
The destiny of one, so vast and true,
Though able to see and follow through.

There is a fork the road now takes,
Which is the road in which to make?
Is it left or to the right?
Will destiny see which is right?

There is a path, a road of life,
The one not taken, a loss despite.
To see what is and to forsake,
The choice is yours, for you must take.

THE PAST ETCHED IN STONE

Past, a time once had been,
Memories, lost within scenes.
Where the ground has been disturbed,
Barren, emptied, and of few words.
Covered over and buried by greens,
A place once here many have seen.
The walls grew, each placed by stone,
Perfected, then whose time left alone.
Hands in place with gentle care,
Years have passed yet it's still there.
Buried by time and left alone,
A path once beaten now overgrown.
The walls rise, seem square in shape,
Hand-ladened stones still crumble away.
Still the home remains, lost over time,
Memories of those destined through time.
For below the ground, buried beneath,
No voice of time, unable to speak.
Walls fell away, waiting for the day,
One to discover, a time passed away.

THERE STOOD A HOUSE

Many years or so it's been,
For some but few have ever seen.
The place we knew sometime before,
Has fallen to ruins, treasured once more.
Trees of old now hide the way,
Crowding the path, many a day.
Memories of time, shared by all,
Few who cared, cherished recalled.
Curtains in the window, tattered, torn,
Wooden porch now withered and worn.
Upon the shelf, a layer of dust,
A broken picture, memory of such.
Land is parched, choked by disease,
Tall grasses and vines amongst the weeds.
Smell of smoke within the walls,
The sky is dark, heavy rain falls.
The fire ravaged the vacant lands,
Only the fireplace, vacant still stands.
Charred wood and smoke remain,
Memories of lives, lost in the flames.
Within each aspect, a part of life,
Doused by water, the flames are out.
Within the ashes, the memories of mine,
Lost in the moment, through time.

WHERE THE RIVER TURNS

As the river that winds its way,
Around each corner, the beauties displayed.
Upon the river, it's deep and wide,
All that it holds, the will to abide.
As the greenery that lines its way,
Nature's wonder, it changes each day.
When the speed is slower, sometimes fast,
As the picture in life that's grasped.
As the river at times, it's still,
In the waters, nature has willed.
As it slows, there is more life around,
Just look inside and see life is found.
For the river this way it flows,
As each day it differs and grows.
When it turns, the current that flows,
Slows the journey, the river still grows.

CHAPTER 8
COVID-19 PANDEMIC

A PATH CHOSEN FOR INSPIRATION, A TOKEN

The hours it seems within these walls,
Days and nights, I am beginning to crawl.
The noise, the kids, the sounds I hear,
Too much, too soon, I must leave here.
To find a place, some time alone,
A place to go, to be on my own.
To breathe, to relax, to take a breath,
To be alone, with no ill regrets.
To take a walk, a chance to breathe,
To the great outdoors, a sight to see.
And down the road, a path chosen,
A place to wander, my voice has spoken.
Upon the path, the road I choose,
As it winds its way, I cannot lose.
It is to remember, to do my part,
Social distancing just six feet apart.
To find a space, where few are found,
To search and find, where no one's around.
To follow the path, that winds its way,
Over the hill, this place to play.
Along the path, there is a stone or two,
With a word expressed, colourful too.
Words to advise, words with heart,
A feeling of loneliness, as were all apart.
A thoughtful note, with paint displayed,
A magical task, as small ones say.
With paint and words, a spirit will rise,
That feeling within, you soon realize.

Just a word and set in place,
A warmer feeling you now embrace.
And on this path, another lies,
One other saying with colourful ties.
The thought, a feeling, to be apart,
Yet disconnected to do their part.
Within a smile, within one stone,
The road now chosen; you are not alone.

WAITING TO GET MY SHOT IN THE ARM

Each day, I ponder and speak aloud,
How long do I wait, what about now?
The virus takes a life, perhaps it's mine,
How long do I wait, will there be time?
I wash my hands and Purell to a scent;
The cash I lay out, every red cent.
I wear my mask, the lines on my face;
My tan lines will show and mark my fate.
The more I converse seemly not is rude;
My lips are chapped, Vaseline to soothe.
Watching the news, they deliver and debate;
The number seemingly rising, marking my fate.
The cases rise each day, I'm closer still;
A chance to breathe, ease my broken will.
Vaccines arrive for those nearly dead;
I'm not old enough to share daily bread.
The word on the street, a shot in the arm;
The side effects are worse, it can do no harm.
Whether green or orange or red and grey,
The forecast is changing, every day.
A visit to a store, I take in stride;
To pick and choose, I still have my pride.
The cases increased, a variant will change;
I am playing so nice, I'm still playing the game.
A sudden break as the population's changes;
The age that I have reached, I'm still in the game.
To register online or even place a call;
Countless hours spending, waiting above all.

Fifteenth place, I have registered hours it takes;
Waiting and wondering, perhaps it's fate.
Endless minutes, hours, days it seems;
Now even closer, only once was a dream.
Weeks go by without even a sign;
Frustration takes hold, I'm out of time.
I walked into the pharmacy, to my chagrin,
And asked the pharmacist, can I check in?
I waited and watched, inquiring a sign;
Just fill out the form and checking each line.
Take a seat, just waiting for a sign;
Fifteen minutes flew by, I sat in the chair.
A jab in the arm, the excitement was there;
Fifteen minutes I waited, and watched in haste;
Perhaps only now, four more months I now wait.

COME TOGETHER RIGHT NOW SIX FEET AWAY

The screen is now fuzzy,
The signal barely there.
All is dark and hazy,
To view were now aware.

We look at the screen,
To see what we miss.
To hold someone close,
A moment to reminisce.

A gaze into a world,
A view from within.
The screen now opens,
Our lives now begin.

We look into a home,
A space they now share.
Observe what is on the walls,
The view was now aware.

Upon the wall, trinkets hang,
A look into this scene.
For all they want to be,
Objects as they have been.

A portrait, one picture,
A moment lost in time.
The scene of a family,
Together, makes them shine.

Together, at one time,
A moment, as it seems.
Filling the minutes each day,
Remembering how to dream.

We work to make a living,
To provide for our means.
Our kids are still learning,
Differences is what it seems.

We are all working together,
To find a reason to be.
Our lives ever so busy,
This end will we see.

All these faces are here,
So many fill the space.
Talking, laughing, and sharing,
Moments to share our place.

To share a few moments,
To voice and converse.
To remember the old feeling,
Yet hard to find the words.

Facetime, Instagram, and Twitter,
iPhone, Android, and Zoom.
Laptops, iPads, and emails,
We welcome all into our room.

The screen now closes,
All is black and white.
Images now all fade,
No longer in the light.

The inability to hug,
Or shake a hand.
To be so close,
I still do not understand.

FOUNDATIONS WITHIN A DESIRE

I wake and rise to see a new day,
A chance, one choice, yet only today.
A new day, a delight, besides,
A chance, a change, soon realized.

To wash and shower, to bathe perhaps,
To dress, to appear, for I will not lapse.
Upon my face, a foundation will rise,
Adding more makeup, a colour to decide.

Then the blush, a warming shade,
To colour and blend, a softening trade.
Upon my lips, a colour choice,
What shall I wear, my inner voice?

Perhaps it's red or yellow or green,
A change perhaps, a festive scene.
Upon my eyes, a liner will prove,
A bold colour and nothing to lose.

The eyes, the shadow, a softer tone,
To brush and layer and go it alone.
To crimp the lashes, oh, what a pain,
For long and lush, beauty to refrain.

To look in the mirror and one last glance,
To change my mind, to have a chance.
And don my mask, to disguise this all,
Hours it seems, and to protect us all.

WHEN CAN I GET A SHOT IN THE ARM FOR REAL?

I wake each morning and look to the skies,
To wish for a happier place, until I realize.

This day is beginning, just another one,
Just as yesterday, has ended for some.

To get up and move, it's hard to try;
And with each day, despair in disguise.

Now I need food and eat, for my sake;
The kids must be fed and stay awake.

To use, to shop the ordinary way;
Go into and shop, in the aisles my way.

To look and find the items I need;
To spend my cash, is what I believed.

To use a tablet, laptop, or phone;
Now remember the app. I am so alone.

To use a tool that frightens me away;
I must learn to shop, still I'm afraid.

A password is needed, where or when?
I need my normal ways; will this end?

I fumble through notes and upon the page;
My list of passwords is now displayed.

The items I chose and meals to create;
The snacks to order are in great debate.

I chose the items for which I need;
Now paying perhaps, I still disagree.

I wish for cash, it's my only means;
Asking to help paying, charging it seems.

A knock at the door, the time has arrived,
To walk to the door, as my walker decides.

The food has arrived, hungry kids await,
To prepare the meals, a healthy debate.

Those of us, still work from home;
Strapped to the chair, no office to roam.

Though half my body is dressed to show,
The bottom half, my pjs flow.

The kids are fed, unto the tablets they learn;
Are they understanding, this is my concern.

Away from the class and missing their friends;
To ask for assistance, an in-person friend.

For a tablet, laptop, desktop, or phone;
And now to Zoom, I feel so alone.

To check the Internet, to find a way;
The upload speed seems so far away.

The power goes out, our devices go down;
A loss of productivity, an unending sound.

Don the jackets, scarves, mitts, and hats;
To go for exercise, for recess at last.

To stroll in the neighbourhood, go for a walk;
To see the outdoors, excitement has brought.

To wash our hands, twenty seconds in all;
The use of disinfectant, a new normal evolved.

My hands are dry, cracked, and sore;
Perhaps more lotion, now to order a chore.

To wipe things down, to spray and disinfect;
Garbage is mounting, and costs I didn't expect.

To prepare a snack and healthy treats;
Fresh fruits and vegetables our bodies seek.

Homework is needed and meals to prep;
Coffee, tea, and a drink, what's next?

Dinner is prepped and finally cleaned,
To watch a Netflix movie and snacking it seems.

To Zoom with friends, a chance to recall;
So many faces to remember one and all.

Many faces and voices that want to speak;
To wait and watch, a chance we seek.

Some things not missed, and most of all,
Fighting the traffic and hours, we crawl.

To hop on a bus, a cab, or train;
To find a seat, and never complain.

To meet up with friends, a social event;
To eat inside, this moment, we spent.

To book a vacation, some time away;
Go on an adventure, a chance to play.

As the numbers decrease, we welcome you all;
To celebrate a birthday, only ten people called.

We gather around, in a circle to park;
Six feet away, we do not embark.

A disguise we wear, to hide our face;
To hold back the germs and mask our place.

The cake is chosen, and now is bought;
A moment to wish, and one final thought.

To blow out the candles, a wonderful thought;
My germs are spread, the cake we tossed.

Each day we wait and watch the news;
The numbers are rising to mixed reviews.

The vaccine is found, an encouraging thought;
Millions still hope this will not stop.

When can I get my shot in the arm?
Will it last, and do no harm?

GETTING A SHOT IN THE ARM, THE NEXT DAY REGRETS

AstraZeneca vaccine was the shot of choice;
No concern from me, in a thankful voice.
I dozed off to bed and wondered, what's next;
120 days to wait, seemed so perplexed.

The cost was reasonable, no cash in hand;
I left the pharmacy feeling so grand.
I pondered the thought, how long to wait;
Checking emails, my appointment's a debate.

I wake and wonder, what have I done;
The vaccine that I've received, feeling I'm done!
The one shot I waited and wondered, what next;
The pain in my shoulder, I soon became vexed.

The pain in my arm is sensitive and sore;
Rolling over in bed, I regretted this chore.
Woke up weak, indeed, thought I was through;
I stumbled to my feet; damn, I had the flu.

Weakened and tired, this shot I deserved;
I thought for a moment, &$%# in one word.
My weakened state, a moment had dawned;
A Ferris Bueller moment, soon it was gone.

Calling in sick, a thought crossed my mind;
Momentary loss of reasoning, retired shined.
I summoned the nurse; though Lisa had arrived;
Destined for movement, soon resigned.

I searched for bruising, and to my dismay,
The bus that hit me left me in disarray.
No bones were broken, no bruising had shown;
Yet still reeling in pain, a shot I now owned.

The fever soon broke, the sheets now wet;
A shower I earned, washing sheets, regret.
The arm was sore, tender to the touch;
Should I change my view now, not so much.

Lethargic and weak, still unable to play,
I slept and recovered an undaunting day.
Weakened, distraught, a moment occurred:
Was it just the shot, this I deserved?

I review my medications, wondering aloud,
Was it just side effects or the shot somehow?
Checked the site and reviewed the effects;
Damn, I was right, to my regret.

Four months to go, to wait and wonder;
Get another shot and day to be under.
Perhaps one day, a distant time
We drive into normalcy, happier we shine.

In the days to come, appointments I'd placed,
Asking to come in to get vaccinated debate.
One by one, these messages soon revealed;
Most of them, I pondered, wasn't a big deal.

ISOLATION, HOW LONG WILL IT LAST?

A feeling of loss, the emptiness has brought,
Stillness haunts this place.
Alone it seems, the long-awaited dreams,
When can we leave this space?
Darkness surrounds, the unavoidable abounds,
To fill these hours at home.
As the walls close in, uneasiness begins,
Friends once found, we're now alone.
To find a mask, or dare I ask,
Where are they to be found?
I look online, or walk the line,
To live this life without bounds.
With gloves and Purell, a new life dwell,
Toilet paper above all the rest.
Disinfect and clean, life as it seems,
We wonder in the months what's next.
We wander the aisles, emptiness for miles,
The supplies once plentiful now gone.
Limitless of food, for the endless brood,
A culture, where did we go wrong?
Spring has sprung, planting has begun,
Yet limits to the workers are lost.
The border forbids, workers that would give,
Their time to aid the distraught.
The needs of all, the economy might fall,
Above all, we are all aware.
This virus can kill, it has no will,
Doctor, nurses, in our hospitals care.
A drought of time, the necessity to find,

The words we so often share.
This feeling seems, as a human being,
My thoughts, I now must bear.
Once gathered as friends, the time we'd spend,
To laugh and to share about life.
We call or text, FaceTime, what's next,
Distancing is nothing without a fight.
With movies galore, my eyes are now sore,
Countless hours it all seems.
Now up to date and willing to debate,
Life as we know it, not without dreams.

STILL THE MOVEMENT NOW, 2020

What to expect, another year no less,
This virus it still will not quit.
As we shutter at home, no place to roam,
Frustrations are making me sick.

Many hours we spend, our devices lend,
Distractions to live and learn.
Zoom and express, on learning we expect,
Yet snacking is still a concern.

The excessive weight, as our midriff waits,
A choice just to get exercise.
Calories to burn, an ongoing concern,
The clubs we wish we could decide.

As the numbers rise, upwards to the skies,
A vaccine may be close at hand.
A stab in the arm, can do no harm,
Another twenty-eight days do we stand.

Millions we wait, still lying we debate,
Will this be the only one?
Patiently we strive, keeping healthy and alive,
Yet still dying to succumb.

We wait for a test, many hours no less,
To see if we are all okay.
Positively we fight, for negative we delight,
Each day begins, as we now pray.

The morning news, depressing we lose,
For those who will not succumb.
The cases still climb and the warning signs,
Perhaps the end will never come.

We dare not fall or break bones at all,
For the hospital we dare not arrive.
To take one step, PPE they stress,
For tomorrow we hope, we're still alive.

I love to shop, a moment had brought,
And don a mask to wear.
Breathing is a pain, fogging up I disdain,
My blast shield deflects germs out there.

Purell I now wear, a cologne I share,
The smell seems to get around.
Fragrance fills the air, and all are aware,
The shelves are emptied I have found.

We shop with space, long times we wait,
The shelves are empty as well.
We grin and bear and expense, it's not fair,
To feed our families for a spell.

Many months we wait, the vaccine to debate,
Will the rest of us get a shot?
Can we see our friends, dinner out to spend?
Going back to school will rock.

Gathering once more, BBQ is no chore,
The ability just to have fun.
Our sanity we strive, to go outside,
To walk, to jog, or just to run.

A moment to ponder, a while longer,
To book some time away.
A vacation perhaps, as time will lapse,
To cruise and the time to stay.

Memories we still share, are lost somewhere,
For a time before this all began.
One day we'll be asked, a moment will pass,
Recollect and remember to take a stand.

As the years progress, taken lightly no less,
Our lives will reflect from the past.
What we expect, to follow each step,
For our history, this tool will lapse.

WHAT'S NEXT, 2022?

How to cope, thoughts invoke;
Another year has come and gone.
COVID's here to stay, the ability to walk away;
Another shot and something feels wrong.

Each morning I rise, look up to the sky,
To see what has changed.
I turn on the news, the paper to peruse,
Cases of COVID are the same.

We live under the dome, no place to roam,
Venture outside for a break.
Unlock the door, my PPE cannot ignore,
Disinfecting is not a mistake!

How long can it last, my ability to grasp,
Unknown how long it is here.
To plan an escape, pack the car for a break,
A vacation, a reality, is feared!

Disinfect hands and face, two masks in place,
Saving time, for beauty remains.
New lines they conceal, the mask reveals,
Reminded daily, I'm still the same.

Breathing's a chore, glasses fogging more,
The string on the mask seems tight.
Force of the mask, my confidence is dashed,
The challenges are an endless fight.

Hidden by disguise, I soon realize,
My friends I may not recall.
We pass on the road, not recognizing, I suppose,
When we meet, I may forget them all.

I follow the rules, I'm back in school,
Routine is always the same.
I wake from the dream, every night it seems,
A roulette wheel that never changed.

Dare I go outside, perhaps it's goodbye,
For this year it's almost done.
I wait for the day, precious time away,
Unmasked, a celebration for everyone.

RETURN TO SENDER

How long does it take, many months to forsake?
A solution is nowhere in sight.
On foreign soil, a virus takes a toll,
Is there a remedy that we can fight?

This virus was created, and never debated,
What is the reason why?
What have we learned, never-ending concern?
How many more must die!

In the air we breathe, invisible, we cannot see,
Yet this virus is carried to all.
Across the vast seas into our homes, now believed,
Infecting us one and all.

On the front lines, our health care is defined,
Hospitals and their ability to fight.
Like a great storm, we were never informed,
One by one, we lose our right.

Millions spent to find, many on the front lines,
The toll on lives is great.
The family we have lost, what is the cost,
Now there is a real debate!

Elderly, ability to survive, the virus takes lives,
Doctors and nurses who need to rest.
Long hours they work, lives to preserve,
Exhausted to the point of death.

The new rules defined, we wait in lines,
Long hours, days, and weeks.
A shot in the arm, can do no harm,
Our reaction and ability to defeat.

We disinfect our lives, as the virus thrives,
Masking the reason, to the extreme.
One shot we wait, months in haste,
Waiting, a second time to be seen.

A loss of wage, stressed, we age,
Depression is at an all-time high
The cost of food, to feed our brood,
The answer when we will decide.

VOLUNTEERING A SENSE OF PRIDE

There is just one, she is important too,
Her struggle to wage, her instinct to prove.
Within her dreams, a chance to strive,
Searching within the understanding still lies.
All that she is, in that she shares,
All that she holds, her feelings are aware.
In others that she speaks, her sense of being,
A caring, perhaps, is the volunteering.
A sense of pride for those she's shown,
Her ability to prove, in that she's grown.
With her tasks, her devotion sets forth,
Knowing in her heart, Maria sets her course.
With the smile, the frown is gone,
Newfound accomplishment, a sense to belong.
With the feeling inside, the direction is found,
The path is chosen, the growing is allowed.

CHAPTER 9
REMEMBERING, HOW TO

HEAVING SPHERICAL OBJECTS TO TARGET

Upon the floor, shoes, the ability to score,
High style, there is no doubt,
With aid and ease, no grip you see,
The ability to slide about.

High-gloss shine, in comfort sometimes,
Perhaps there is no need,
Fashion fazed, the sixties craze,
This aim is what it's believed.

With no disguise, no arch to rise,
Comfort, some might agree,
To extend the life, the floors, shined, ignite,
With style and grace comes speed.

The floor of oak, with sheen of gold,
Polished to a high-gloss shine,
Each board is selected and lines perfected,
Science will work in time.

The ball is round, circular it found,
With holes found in one place,
Within three holes, the fingers take hold,
To hurl it into space.

Each colour scheme a science, a means,
Each one a hidden weight,
The choice you reside, you must decide,
Your ability is now the debate.

One choice to make, to have and forsake,
Decide which foot goes first,
A rhythmical dance, now one last chance,
Now you can do no worse.

To grasp the ball, a hesitation to recall,
Three fingers into the holes,
Arch the arm, moving forward to disarm,
And let that sucker roll.

Unto the floor, the distance spans,
Just sixty feet away,
Just hurl the ball unto the lane,
Just hope and wish and pray.

Sudden thump upon the floor,
The ball an uncertain end,
The targets in sight, now wait and watch,
To collide to a bitter end.

To count the pins, to take a turn,
A chance to do no wrong,
To make a spare, perhaps a strike,
This feeling inside grows strong.

Nine more tries to get it right,
To bowl a perfect game,
A spare, a strike, or just to par,
Having fun is just the same.

RIDING A BIKE; A RENEWED SENSATION

Upon the ground, a rapid pace,
A smiling child can never replace.
Two wheels, a frame, handlebars, and seat,
The tubular steel, fun cannot defeat.
For many years, too many perhaps,
Just riding a bike, the time has lapsed.
Three years it's been searching around,
Looking for a bike that cannot be found.
Searching online and in a bike store,
Colour, size, shape, the endless chore.
Checking out ads, shopping around,
The endless journey, frustrations found.
A conversion sparked, a neighbourly friend,
A new cycling company, enthusiasm did lend.
To research a bike, many miles from home,
To a county and origin, the language unknown.
A call was placed, questions were asked,
The bikes were sized, shipped at last.
The day has arrived, the box reveals,
Just two long years, shiny new wheels.
The price and style and just in time,
To exercise, a fight, a pound at a time.
To stretch and strain, to flex and grow,
How to ride, to remember we're not alone.
Helmet to protect our skull from harm,
The shorts, with cushions, the tush conform.
Lights in front, back to be seen,
A bell that sounds and warns it's me!

Whether it be a traditional wheel,
Or a racer for the wind that he feels.
Or a banana seat, a cool style,
Getting out for a ride for a while.

SPECTACLES THROUGH THE LOOKING GLASS

A change in life, these years despite,
The eyes seem tired somehow.
To look at a page, to squint in dismay,
Glasses to magnify the letters now.

Further it seems, the letters have been,
Once they seemed so clear.
The years progress, distance even less,
Smaller in size is what I fear.

The lights are dim, a change within,
Age seems to trick the eyes.
A throbbing in the head, headaches I dread,
Fuzziness, a change in disguise.

As night closes in, the eyesight dims,
A halo seems to arise.
A ghosting effect, the strain no less,
Correcting the vision, one tries.

A visit to the store, with spectacles galore,
Many shapes, sizes, and styles.
Hundreds on the wall, designers, one and all,
Sticker shock changes all the while.

A phoropter, a device, exacting and precise,
Lenses to refract your sight.
Each lens reveals, refracting to reveal,
Determine the prescription is right.

A test to reveal, the ability to conceal,
A Snellen chart hangs on the wall.
The letters are arranged, smaller they remain,
A view, a challenge to us all.

The eye tests, an annual respect,
Tropicamide drops to dilute the eyes.
A sting to reveal, the pupils concealed,
The ability to look in the eye.

Those with medical concerns, the ophthalmologist learns,
Looking into the eyes for a change.
Avoid disease, early onset he sees,
Checking out the inner eye veins.

A thought to collect and not regret,
A way to keep glasses at bay.
In the case, or on your face,
A loss for insurance may not pay.

A decision, a plight, a decision, a right,
Contacts is a means to see.
The ability to try and insert in the eye,
A target too small to believe.

Cut to the chase, a daily pair to replace,
A new pair each day awaits.
A new set of eyes, colouring may disguise,
Tinted contacts to coordinate.

Those with flair have several pairs,
To coordinate with each day's attire.
Specks, shades, blinkers, cheaters, or peepers,
At the end of day seeing, we desire.

We all partake, seeing life we forsake,
Getting older is a change we've seen.
Glasses get us through, this we cannot lose,
A speckle, this life has been.

THE LOVE OF SNOW, OR JUST SHOVING IT!

A question was posed, an idea arose,
Shovelling snow is a feat!
The ability to partake, have, and forsake,
The cooling sensation a real treat.

Perhaps for most, the effort, a toast,
Cold weather a cooling treat.
Better to shovel snow when it's cold
Than to cut the lawn in the heat.

It's a wonderful season, no rhyme or reason,
Cold temperatures know no bounds.
When zero is seized, negativity disagrees,
Ability to adapt gets some down.

With layers to defend, the cold to spend,
This daunting task has limits.
Keeping warm, a feat, just walking to defeat,
Moving a challenge, just a bit!

The tools desired, strong muscles required,
The ability to stand in the snow.
If the budget is lean, a shovel is seen,
Hours of work still blows!

A device is desired, as costs run higher,
Snow blowers, gas-guzzling machines.
The skill required to drive the desire,
To cut time down by any means.

The lucky few, with driveways to pursue,
Many cars have a place to stay.
The hours you spend, a path to defend,
Mounds of snow in which to play.

Morning, you arise, to sunny blue skies,
A chance to get to work on time remains.
Snowplows had gone by, the end of the drive,
A wall of ice, to your disdain.

Winter is bleak, warm weather we seek,
Fewer layers and warmth remain.
All those retired, with comfort, a desire,
Deidre, shovelling snow, a young person's game.

THE ABILITY TO TALK AND NOT TEXT

How to describe what I see with my eyes,
Technology that others cannot grasp.
The sign of the times, for one final time,
Perhaps I'm one of the last.

The ability to speak, for others who reap,
A design and way to talk.
Invention to create, ability to communicate,
A genius's way was thought.

The creator in the voice, each but a choice,
Transmitting words over wires.
A harmonic telegraph, as some who laugh,
The invention of the phone inspired.

The box on the wall, described by all,
A device with a means to speak.
A circle encased numbers that illuminate,
Dialling with a finger, a real treat.

Changing of the times, some with a party line,
Those of us who experience this phone.
Listening for the ring, two long, one thing,
The way to communicate from home.

As the population grew, the phone did too,
The numbers once dialled were so few.
Later in years, the area code appears,
Now dialling eleven numbers grew.

Sign of the times, a memory of mine,
Explaining to the kids of today.
Just stand by the wall, dial for a call,
You cannot run away.

CHAPTER 10
IN THE DARK

A CLOSE ENCOUNTER OF AN ALIEN KIND

The sky was black, no light would attract,
No movement, no sound, a void.
Perhaps in a daze, glass-eyed, arrayed,
A voice awoke me from my node.

A light appeared, close, not near,
Though asleep, soundly, I awoke.
For in the sky, a light did fly,
Something strange, we'd seen it both.

Beyond the dark, an object embarked,
Beyond the canyons so deep.
For in the sky, a craft did fly,
So broad, bold, and sleek.

Beyond the range, light so strange,
Beyond the sea of stars.
For on this night, there came a light,
Something so near, yet far.

The light but one, one other succumbed,
Yet bright white and round.
No sounds did rise, as it flew on by,
The origin not ours was found.

Circular, perhaps, distance did lapse,
Strange how it broke the sky.
In this a void, the craft had toyed,
We gazed as it flew on by.

There seemed but one, another would succumb,
Still faster, it hesitated then stayed.
In a blast to speed, the second did heed,
In learning it found its way.

A moment to recall, witnessing above all,
These two lights did appear.
They rose and fell, then glided a spell,
Almost close, yet distant it neared.

It streaked across the sky, it hovered, then dived,
It hung motionless, at ease.
A second craft moved closer, inching its way close,
Rising upward with ease.

These two would gaze, amazement with array,
Their eyes, they could not part.
Perhaps in the proof, unable they viewed,
To look they'd miss this part.

As one did speak, the other agreed,
To the right then to the left.
Each change was seen, other eyes agreeing,
For what was to be the next.

The crafts graced the sky, and dashed on by,
They moved, remained so still.
One craft would lead, the other did heed,
In a move, vanishing over the hill.

A second lapsed, the craft did pass,
Moving vertically to the sky.
A moment to pause, taking in what was,
We'd sit, wait, and wonder why.

In the distance, it passed, we squinted to grasp,
The sight before our eyes.
Form was unknown, an unfriendly form,
It came into our lives.

Perhaps only to some, these friends did come,
Who's to say they are wrong.
A chosen few, a change to view,
Unto our galaxy . . . and beyond.

AS DARKNESS FILLED THE ROOM, DARK NIGHT

On this night, a lack of light,
The darkness now settles in.
The voices arose, as did the smoke,
The eve, the night, now begins.

Hidden just inside, eager souls did thrive,
The night was now to start.
Upon this night, the stars shone bright,
Within each a warming heart.

Within the crowd, the noise seemed loud,
The candles so few and less.
The smoke rolled in, time would begin,
The start was anyone's guess.

The time did pass to converse, at last,
Decisions were soon to be made.
In the dark, these souls embarked,
The games we'd heed were played.

Within this time, the room would shine,
Few candles the light had eased.
With the smoke that billowed and choked,
The people, the crowd, was pleased.

Soon, after eight, all would vacate,
The bar a place to play.
On the road, these ones took hold,
Soon we were on our way.

Games were played, bars we stayed,
This night, this time was late.
The eve did call, this team recalled,
To win this place was fate.

DARK IS THE NIGHT

Though all seems black and no way back,
To set forth is to journey ahead.
So daring and true to follow through,
Does one ever dread?

For one is there, though unaware,
Seeing one cannot part.
To look inside, as one does cry,
Seeing is impossible in the dark.

No light to see, no motion a scene,
Set forth no sign to move.
Does one embark unto the dark,
To venture and go on through.

A sense to roam, to fend from home,
To stumble, to motion on forth.
Reaching with hands, try to understand,
The direction and on due course.

Slow is the walk, silence is to talk,
To feel, to find a way.
To shed some light, rid the fright,
Struggling to work out a way.

IT CAME IN THE NIGHT

For in the woods, beyond the stream,
The mist hung heavy and low.
On this night, the moon shone bright,
The mood ebbed and flowed.

In the fog, over bushes and logs,
The light shone from within.
In the light, the haze was bright,
Something moved in the wind.

Down the path, overgrown, it lacked,
The way was no longer clear.
The forest had grown, seeds now sown,
The light shone its way near.

Trees did rise to wayward sky,
Branches reached out from above.
For on this night, came a light,
It appeared silently from above.

The light grew bright, steady, and white,
Moving even closer it neared.
The form had ceased, a sense of peace,
This night the form had appeared.

A voice that spoke, our minds awoke,
All seemed quiet and still.
For it had come, appearing for some,
And graced us with its will.

The light was warm, it changed its form,
The message it had sent.
It disappeared, no longer from here,
On that night a moment we spent.

The time belonged, the mood was gone,
All seemed still and at ease.
But these ones unsure what had come,
Wondering why did it leave?

SOMETHING IN THE MIST

In the mist, there is a soul,
Without a voice, feeling is the cold.
Within the haze, an image appears,
Lurking in the depths, its presence is near.

Upon the light that breaks the night,
Though emptiness, the darkness reveres.
The dim light glows, the eeriness flows,
Imagination takes in the fear.

Perhaps a spell, the victim's dwell,
The direction which is right.
Perhaps the left, for which is next,
Though chosen would destine our plight.

As one sensed cold, the other controlled,
The mood would set the scene.
For within this night, a fear, a delight,
This dwelling, the night had been.

Two such souls began to stroll,
As now the night drew near.
For one had seen the illusions had been,
The distance so vast was feared.

For two souls the night took hold,
Their plight in the hands of one.
A sudden mistake, a sense forsaken,
For in the mist, it had begun.

A stroll, a walk, these voices talked,
Yet something inside had changed.
A time yet unaware, something was there,
The feeling grew stronger was changed.

A voice did speak, one politely agreed,
A question to a solution was best.
A helpful soul, as two did know,
With thanks the moment was blessed.

Warmth of the mall, the elements did fall,
The heat, a warming treat.
To walk with care, to have been there,
To wander, to watch, to see.

Against the crowd, these two were allowed,
To enter and exit with ease.
To wander around, new sights and sounds.
To move about as they pleased.

One moment was feared, so close, so near,
The door that opened was closed.
The moment grew near, fate seemed near,
No means, no road, no key.

A moment of haste, an erratic pace,
The door and freedom would wait.
Into the cold, to wander, to know,
The time, the past, would wait.

Unto the night, the haze, the delights,
The fog, the cold two souls.
The emptiness arose, the fear took hold,
The moment that eve, the cold.

In the fog, the image was gone,
In the silence, it had since moved on.
Shrouded in the mist, a feeling missed,
For on the moment, the warmth arose.

Feelings were shared, hesitations aware,
Moments renewed sense of being.
Looking for the signs, knowing in time,
Waiting for the next-time feelings.

THE FIRE INSIDE

Within just a spark, the air lets it grow,
It ignites with fear, a warmth we all know,
Within a storm, the light may strike,
A crackle of fear, leaving a devastating fight.

In the distance, there is a light,
Breaks on the horizon, it hides in the night,
It burns within, inside there is a glow,
It's triggered by heat, within, it only knows.

Within it strikes fear and glows in the dark,
Warms when it is near, within the heart,
Inside there is fear, something that it hides,
It comes in the light; with air it thrives.

An animal that is feared and strikes out so near,
Within there is a life, destroys all who are here,
A life that takes control has no heart, no soul,
Having no bounds, no fear, it's glowing near.

CHAPTER 11
NORTH FOLK

AUTUMN LEAVES

The autumn leaves seem no more,
Nothing's left but a vacant shore.
Stillness has taken over this land,
Signs of winter are here to stand.

Wild birds have come and gone,
To the south from where they belong.
As the squirrels gather up their food,
Before the snow and cold there too.

The days turn cold and the nights short,
Few walk the road of a different sort.
The smell of burning leaves, a fragrance soar,
The smoke ascends, rises no more.

Brightly coloured leaves have faded away,
The cool feeling has taken over today.
The autumn colours have ceased to be,
Once colourful splendour for autumn leaves.

Once was fall, winter has now come,
Chilling to the bone, too soon for some.
Still some leaves cling to the trees,
For months from now, spring will release.

All that autumn once lived ceases,
And as the cold the once warmed agrees.
Except the ones who brave the cold,
Few who hoped for warmth the winter stole.

Each day the snow comes this way,
Winter's breath has dawned today.

A PLACE ONCE VISITED, THESE FEELINGS ARE AWARE

I travelled this road, too long I suppose,
Up the crest and over the rise.
I was looking for a sign, it's been sometime,
To the heavens, up to the sky.

The road had a bend, onward to the end,
Suddenly a presence I felt, only now!
The warmth surrounds, unknowing I'd found,
A presence had greeted me somehow.

A voice spoke, my thoughts awoke,
Someone I still remember, only now.
The light grew bright, glowing white,
My memory still lapses somehow.

A sensation from within, eerily like the wind.
A feeling I was drawn to the door.
Turn and walk in, a cold feeling begins,
I felt this feeling once more.

A light did appear, as if someone was here,
A light not seen for some time.
Upon the chair, a cross that bears,
An angel whose presence still shines.

A light did appear, vivid yet unclear,
A shadow, its presence now aware.
A candle shone bright, a flickering light,
Memories of past resigned there.

This feeling seems lost, a distant thought,
Many years this sensation stirred within.
A voice I had heard, conversing words,
A loss I still bear deep now begins.

Now drawn to the shore, again once more,
A sensation felt stronger even now.
I followed the path, over the rocks and back,
Then stopped and hesitated just now.

I found a chair, though barely there,
The colour now faded and worn.
Once it would ignite, and shone so bright,
The warmth an infectious form.

Wandering to the edge, the step I'd dread,
The height unbearable even now.
The bridge had a bend, uncertainty would lend,
I was determined to cross it somehow.

Trees would surround, as autumn did abound,
The colours too many to see.
Upon this land, a sacred soul stands,
Guarding it for all who still believe.

Perhaps just one voice, only to have a choice,
To guard over all that we see.
To protect and share, for all who dare,
A place inside and we still believe.

BALA . . . A TIME NOT FORGOTTEN, 2020

There's a place up north that steers our course,
A place so familiar to go.
Where streams collect, our memoirs reflect,
This place that few people know.

Fond memories are shared, our family is there,
Once a year, we finally arrive.
For some of us, who never give up,
The Bala Cranberry Festival decides.

Thirty-five years it's been, yet hard it seems,
A few more grey hairs reside.
The change in season, for only one reason,
These faces and places will abide.

As the years progress, we all respect,
Age is not on our side.
The grey hairs turn and aches a concern,
A little patience now sets our stride.

This tart little fruit, bitter taste to boot,
With jams, muffins, and more.
Thousands who partake, three days to forsake,
Wines and candles galore.

A moment we choose, our diaries will prove,
This sight let some decide.
Our shape and physique, with pride we seek,
This photo we swallow our pride.

Last weekend to reflect, colourful leaves to collect,
Smells of wood burning fill the air.
A dip in the lake, chilly endeavours forsake,
Soon night will dominate the air.

With a sip of wine, we seem to shine,
A dance for all let the spirit free,
With moves you'd swear, old moves with flair,
Moments captured for all to see.

Two months to the day, a phone call away,
A moment of sadness dawned.
The festival is done, for everyone,
The COVID virus ravages on.

THE NIGHT BEFORE THE BALA CRANBERRY FESTIVAL

'Twas the night before the Cranberry Festival all through the town,
Not a vendor was stirring, no decorations were found.
There was no path, not a way cleared,
How would I survive, now lost I feared?
The map that I had was tattered and torn,
Candle wax had melted in weird shapes and forms.
Bala was the town, or so I thought,
Sketches and drawings were all I had brought.
Just north of Gravenhurst, where the Seguin docks,
Just below the surface are dangerous rocks.
The road was unclear, the snow had arrived,
The reindeer were cold and so was I.
A match that I had, the one that I used,
Was covered in snow, and a little wet too.
The wind blew as the match was struck,
Suddenly it was doused, man, I have bad luck.
The clouds soon cleaned, the moon shone bright,
Thanks for the warmth and a shining light.
I followed the map with limited light,
I came upon a dwelling, the beer was in sight.
A light in the window, the curtain was drawn,
Bags of red fruit piled high and beyond.
A young little fellow with bags galore,
Sorted the packages to sell in his store.
A sign in the window, Rooms to Rent,
Exhaustive dedication was worth every cent.
The hour of two and tuckered out was he,
The warmth of the light, a distant memory.

The path that he took, with lantern in hand,
Weaving his way unto a distant land.
Along the road, just near the end,
Two small cottages where the road had a bend.
Sleepy hollow was nestled amongst the trees,
A cabin of logs thwarted the cold breeze.
The crackle of fire, the warmth to forsake,
A warm glass of brandy, inviting one taste.
Aroma of hardwood fills every crevice of time,
A moment to remember, to cherish for all time.
Within a few feet, where the ivy flows,
A cottage of white glistens against the snow.
Through the door, sends a chill to the bone,
The creak of years, the door opens its soul.
With two rooms to lend with cozy attire,
Long-awaited rest and time to retire.
Light of candle is doused and a flicker of red,
A small wisp of smoke now tucked in his bed.

UP NORTH, BALA, A PLACE TO KNOW

There is a place I know, where the cool water flows,
This place where all gather around.
This feeling takes hold, soothing, it slows,
Where family is always around.
Long is the road, many hours we go,
Sights, sounds, and smells appear.
This place called home, a new place to roam,
New beginnings for all that venture here.
The path to find, the way back over time,
The road rises to the crest.
Just over the rise, and before our eyes,
Surprises you will not expect.
So begins the plan, to mould this land,
Others who will want to stay.
To relax and unwind, a slower pace over time,
A place to relax and get away.
All who gather around, a place many have found,
The chosen few make a home.
The struggle to survive, to make a new life,
This place seems far to roam.
Sixty-three years he has stayed, every year to play,
Memories too many to recall.
With a smiling face, and a warming embrace,
Herb welcomes one and all.
Soon the season will end, another year we'll spend,
The Bala Cranberry Festival will call.
Thousands will savour, many newfound flavours,
Enjoyed by one and all.
The smoke will rise, disappear in the sky,

The cool autumn wind now blows.
The chill in the air, as all are aware,
Stillness feeling of winter's cold.
When darkness sets in, the cool winds begin,
For winter will soon be near.
That grip of cold will soon take hold,
Snow will blanket all that is here.
This season will end, and time that we'd spend,
A magical place to stay.
Photos of friends, together again,
Another year we've come to play.

WHERE THE JOURNEY BEGINS, THE BALA WAY

We wait and wonder, we hope and pray,
This place we have found, not far away.
Every year we plan, a place up north,
Three days to relax, to steer our course.
We wait for summer to change its way,
Cooler weather here has come today.
Leaves of green now change their plight,
Yellow, oranges, red, the spirit ignites.
The weather north is always an unknown,
We trek up north, far from home.
Another year has come our way,
Let's celebrate up north, warm place to stay.
Many years, the Bala-Hy we found,
Away from congestion, tranquility surrounds.
A break from reality has come today,
A time to reflect, the northern folk way.
Wind, rain, and sun, we never complain,
We leave with smiles just the same.
We welcome 2021, a special year,
All are welcome, let's give a cheer.
A new broom to whisk today,
A chance to sweep cobwebs away.
Voted the best, where Bala's found,
Smiling faces here, close to town.
To capture, cherish, photograph and respect,
View to pause, a chance to reflect.
Listen and ponder, to wade by the shore,
Walk to explore, to venture once more.

This red fruit, so bitter and sweet,
Grown in marshes, a harvest treat.
Many months of the year, this crop grown,
The land is flooded, the rich sweetness sown.
Vendors who flock to this special place,
To show their wears, a creative space.
A way of life, creations with flair,
Thousands who arrive, a festive affair.
The KEE to Bala, where the music waits,
Sounds of summer, the last weekend awaits.
Motels, hotels, B&Bs booked,
Cool days of autumn are never overlooked.
The Cranberry Festival and a final debate,
Book a golden ticket, thousands await.
Choose a slot, fewer hours to partake,
Will the sun be shining a moment to wait?

CHAPTER 12
FAIRY TALES

THE TOOTH FAIRY

For many years, or so it's been said, the tooth fairy appears when we're asleep in our bed,
Light as a feather, she moves in the night, from house to house, a mission to ignite,
The task at hand, for few of us know, the rule, her duty, now must unfold,
For many do try to reveal this side, only the lucky ones can really fly,
Remember to look and not always stare, her wings are hidden, she's always aware,
She hides them well, they appear at night; with practice, they assist her in flight,
A vote one right, this daunting task reigns, the one who's chosen the goals the same,
A smile for those, a good disposition too, will seal the deal and carry them through,
Warmth within that carries on out, a soul in need, a friend in doubt,
A grasp of life, a cheerful one too, to fit the mould, and a little luck too,
What she brings cannot be shared; she has a gift as all are aware,
It's pride or a sense to share, the honour, the code, the right to bear,
The knowledge, a right, for the task at hand, each size of tooth weighs the demand,
Each tooth a factor to decide the price, the calculation to develop will change her plight,

With size and volume and weight to bear, the cost and price, the currency to share,
Many years in school, many teeth to learn, many sizes to know, ongoing concern,
By day she works, a cause she earns, at night she appears, the love she learns,
Each tooth's a treasure and fought with pain, a space to be filled in minor change,
A look, a smile, a thought, no frowns, she carries her pride and warmth surrounds,
A gift, a moment, a time to share, this task at hand, yet few aren't aware,
A thought, a moment, a time to ask, where does she keep the teeth she brings back?
When does she quit, or does she retire, who's up to the challenge, how does one inquire?
Remember the rule, remember your rights, you have a gift, you bring joy to the night,
Upon each morning, a child will find a coin, a value, to cherish for all time,
A challenge to heed, this goal to share, for one the tooth fairy still cares.

WHEN WILL THE TOOTH FAIRY RETIRE?

The job, the task, the long hours she's trained,
All night long and never complained,
From dusk to dawn, she flies though the night,
Carrying for others is her only plight,
The cash and teeth, she will carry inside,
Sorting and sizing, with confidence and pride,
Through schooling each day, she learns,
Sizes and types and ongoing concern,
During the day, her wings are safe,
Hidden within a special place,
Only at night they can be seen,
Soft and fine of a flossy green,
The floss she shares and remembers to use,
For teeth are precious, we cannot lose,
The loss of a tooth, a sense of shame,
A loss of innocence inside remains,
A toothless smile upon a face,
A photo to remember, a time and place,
Many miles she's travelled, millions more too,
Her ability caring a love through and through,
For on this night, a night we frown,
The tooth fairy we knew is no longer 'round,
The time has come for her to retire,
Many years has it been overdue desire,
The sun has set, and the cold will rise,
To the heavens, above the sky,

The time has come this year to retire,
The love of the job to douse the fire,
The memories we shared a tooth at a time,
A token or two, a memory for all time.

CHRISTMAS CHEER

The sight and sounds, all who surround,
The spirit, the feeling, from within,
Months have passed, Christmas is in our grasp,
The love from inside begins.

It's the time of year we wish great cheer,
For those who perform in voice,
The sounds and smells for all who dwell,
Forsaken, we all make a choice.

All will surround where good friends are found,
The warmth and feelings within,
For what is shared, to have and take care,
The joy of music begins.

Arrangements are made, the words on the page,
Our voices once silenced now rise,
With harmony and grace, love will take place,
Up to the heavens, unto the skies.

With amazing grace, each take their place,
Arranged from young to old,
The hours of fun, memories for some,
And a gift to cherish and hold.

To our gracious hosts who endeavour the most,
To plan a place and decorate,
Countless hours to arrange, they never complain,
To love, to express and tolerate.

A moment to ponder a little while longer,
One special day, we gather one time,
So let us pray for another day,
This moment we all will shine.

THE ELUSIVE EASTER BUNNY

The elusive Easter Bunny, where can he be?
I waited all season and wanted to see.
I was good as gold, I did what was asked,
I did all my chores and never looked back.

I went to search, to look and find,
To search each room over each time.
I looked high and looked low,
Where is he, I will never know.

I followed the map and dotted lines,
I followed the route; the X I will find.
I looked in the closet, under the couch,
Looking for a clue, now I am in doubt.

I looked for the eggs, a trail I know,
I ask a question, does anyone know?
Is he sick or not feeling well?
Is he hiding, or ill for a spell?

Does he have the flu or is he sick?
Is he staying away? Or is this a trick?
I will write a letter and do it real soon,
I do not want to miss, doom and gloom.

I took out my crayons and started to write,
My spelling is horrible, these words I fight.
Dear Easter Bunny, where are you now?
I was good this year, my mom is so proud.

I waited all night and watched the TV,
I read my new book and wanted to believe.
I wanted to see you, but I fell asleep,
You came in the evening, silently you creeped.

I looked for the eggs, none I could see,
Where are they hidden, where can they be?
Did you come to my home and leave a clue?
Were you sick, was it that flu?

Perhaps this year you went away,
Many of my friends, they cannot stay.
I am sad this time and feel alone,
Many of my friends are far from home.

I wrote this letter and still I believe,
Maybe next year, you will come and see.
I will stay awake and hope to find,
An egg or two, Mr. Bunny, you are so kind.

MONKEY BUSINESS; TWINS

Soft and plush and made to share,
The warmth and feeling and made aware.
Cute and cuddly in pink and white,
A child's toy now brought to life.
Soft and warm and always shared,
Two brown and white, a love cared.
A place called home is not far away,
The monkeys' home is now displayed.
Two eyes and a nose and a smile so bright,
The love of a child brings joy and delight.
Softening the tail, a need or desire,
To calm and caress for a little while.
A journey in life, each day at a time,
Carried and treasured, a memory of mine.
Seven years old and growing up fast,
Withered with age, a moment to grasp.
Faded and worn, with a suture or two,
The love of a mother, with a little glue.
Upon the bed, every day and night,
Held close to their hearts, sleep well, good night.

NIGHT BEFORE CHRISTMAS

The night before Christmas,
All about the house,
Mysterious shapes of metal,
Were scattered throughout.

A dusting of white powder,
With a spatula or two,
Tins filled with goodies,
The baking wasn't through.

The fragrance filled the air,
Hidden behind the doors,
The chef hard at work creating,
Cookies, scrumptious treats, and more.

For Santa would be here,
For his sweet goodies one night,
They had to be made,
Mouth-watering, in every bite.

The smell overwhelmed all,
For the morning, we'd wait,
For dessert that evening,
We'd empty the plate.

SANTA'S HELPER

'Twas the night before Christmas and up with a scare,
I dashed to my feet and saw Santa there.
He looked at me strangely, with a gleam in his eye,
Motioned to his elves, take haste, don't be shy.

The squeak in his voice, the sound that he made,
The elves not knowing, they hastened this way.
No voice did he have, no speech he could shout,
No Christmas cheer he could bring, he was all tuckered out.

He said with a squeak, a favour he asked,
Do me this favour, with a warm hearty laugh.
I'm unable to fly, for I have no cheer,
There's a cold in my throat, that's why I'm here!

My look of surprise, for what do I do,
What do I say, with a second or two?
No map that I had, no route I had known,
No license did I have, I'd not even flown.

His arms grabbed me close, he chuckled and moaned,
The smile, his big smile, he laughed as he groaned.
My boy, that he said, no map that you need,
The Elves know their way, good luck and believe.

My pride that I had, I could not say no,
Disappoint Santa? Good heavens, no!
Here's what you say, and remember to laugh,
For here's my secret, for dawn you'll be back.

The list that I had, it's easy to read,
Remember the chimney, for hot it can be.
The presents are listed and colours to match,
For the job is yours, good luck and come back!

With words of wisdom, I took it to heart,
For it's up to me, I'll do my part.
I donned his red suit, though several sizes large, indeed,
With the help of two pillows was all I would need.

I bid Santa adieu, and went on my way,
For unto the night, be off and now pray:
On Dasher, on Dancer, on Prancer, and Vixen,
On Comet, on Cupid, on Donder, and Blitzen!

For unto the night, I sped with ease,
With help from the elves, a gesture I was pleased.
Upon the sled, I drew my hand, and I now swayed,
Upward with a tug, skyward and away.

For upon the night, it was dark stayed,
No thanks to the moon, it lightened my way.
Yet farther below, the ground I could see,
The heights I hated and believe you me.

So far, so high, I'd not look below,
I'd rather not fall, for below there's snow.
For minutes it seemed the roofs were near,
Now worried was I, for landing I feared!

I came down with a thump, the roof I had hit,
I cursed and I swore, I had no cushion to sit!
The wind blew cold and the fire I feared,
My breath that I held, into the black I neared.

Down with a thump, now singed was I,
My hot little tush, I burned my pride.
Unto the stockings, hidden in my sack,
Goodies I had placed in Santa's big sack.

Presents were placed just under the tree,
I tipped-toed so slowly, shh, it's only me.
A warm glass of milk, a cookie or two,
Upon the table, tasteless moo.

I moved to the chimney, waited, now what?
A rope came down, so I climbed up.
Upon the black soot, tight was a squeeze,
No more cookies, thank you, and take the heed.

Up to the cold and unto the sled,
Upwards the sky, northward we sped.
Though more I could tell, the story goes on,
For now, it's late, I must be moving on.

I remembered only now the night of the eve,
I look to the sky and still I believed.
For on that night, many years ago,
I was Santa's Helper, a memory I now know.

The night that I had, the hours were few,
The dawn approached; I was tuckered out too.
A lesson I learned, memory I now store,
The job is difficult, that's what he's for.

I thanked him again, I gestured goodbye,
Away with a dash, northward he'd fly.
Many thanks for the job, the memory I now share,
Merry Christmas to all, good luck, and take care.

WALTER

Grown from a seed among the trees,
Many years of life ahead,
Who would have known a seed once sown,
Would someday be destined to spread?

Plucked from his home by one poor soul,
Eager to look for a tree.
Scrawny it seems, it fits its means,
Once a well-defined tree.

A parcel of land, for there it stands,
Something one can believe in;
Something once sown, many seasons grown,
Something that is seen in him.

Hard as he tried, this his right size,
Though perfect it would be;
A mere two feet tall, to some very small,
For this was Chris's tree.

A place to rest, to gain respect,
Chosen from so many to see;
Its shape and form, so well conformed,
Yet crooked in every degree.

A light below, silent dim glow,
Decorations so little to see;
Tradition set face has taken its place,
Simple and practical it would be.

No lights, no bows, almost nothing glows,
For tradition was to be;
Simple yet true, for all to view
No presents, none of them to see.

CHAPTER 13
KIDS

ANOTHER DAY IN PARADISE; THE COTTAGE

The day had dawned, the sun was bright;
Ice had melted, swimming was a delight.
The sun-yellow hue, warmth in the air;
Running, chasing Rhys, an exhausting affair.
Matty asked Mom if a swim we could go;
We asked Daddy, he wouldn't say no.
We ran into the house a second or two;
Rushing around, no time to lose.
Across the grass and not to destroy;
Grandpa cared for it, it's not a toy.
Down the ramp, yet rough on our feet;
Slowly we walked, swimming is a real treat.
Daddy soon followed, his legs are so long;
Just two short steps, and he's gone.
Closer to the edge, the water is so clear;
I placed my foot in it, colder I feared.
Daddy was patient, yet so slowly he walked;
He hesitated, then he suddenly stopped.
Daddy, I want to watch you go in;
A snicker from Mommy, a feat to begin.
A gasp of air and down to his waist;
Diving in the water, with no haste.
Daddy appears from beneath the lake;
That's a cold one, a shivering debate.
He dashed to his feet and let out a cry;
Daddy, are you okay, this he did not lie.
Mommy motions to Matty, dunk your head;
It's just like a bath before your bed.

Rhys had a plan, I'm not going in;
I'm heading over there, destined to win.
The water is cold and chilled to the bone;
Now Matty's turn, he'd go it alone.
Each step he took, the look of surprise;
Precious to this day, an irresistible eye.
Determined to follow, a dunk in the bay;
Beneath the surface his head stayed.
Shivered and cold, as time did pass;
Rhys was determined, a chance to grasp.
To wade in the water, finally, at last;
His life preserver so snug then a gasp.
He dived into the lake, determined, no fear;
He too was successful, summer now is here.
Crawling over rocks, each step placed;
Scampering for warmth, a loving embrace.

A CHILD, A LIFETIME, AND EXPERIENCE

Born out of love,
Caring so much of,
Since the day she was born.
The time you spent,
Was worth every cent,
You treasure her now even more.

From a tiny child,
Watching her all the while,
Soon she begins to grow.
Though times are trying,
Laughing and crying,
Your heart inside still glows.

For two will share,
One will bear,
The life, the love, but one.
Time will grow,
Love will flow,
The hope, the fears, and fun.

Changing every day,
Growing in every way,
A time you just can't part.
So precious is life,
The love and strife,
A life, a time, a part.

CHRIS GODDARD "SILVERGHOST"

A special bond,
Every day and beyond,
How she changes every day.
A special meaning within,
As her life now begins,
Cherished with love each day.

The day she was born,
The love still warms,
Nothing can ever take it away.
The love you share,
The time you care,
This love grows every day.

She grows up fast,
Time never lasts,
You wonder where it goes.
Days, months, and years,
Through pain and tears,
Times you wish it didn't go,

It's hard not to forget,
The older she gets,
Changes each passing day.
The love and praise,
Time takes away,
This life you share today.

Feelings of change,
Feelings sustained,
Feelings one just can't ease.
Of times and places,
Many new faces,
One time, one chance, a belief.

The years have passed,
The time at last,
She was born just yesterday.
When one so young,
Has now succumbed,
They'll soon be moving away.

BEARING IT ALL

I am a bear, in need or care,
I'm silver and white and soft.
I need a friend, some warmth to lend,
To trust, to share, to talk.

A little love, shares a hug,
To bare, to wonder, to hold.
Think of me when I can't be.
In times when the warmth turns cold.

Please wipe my tears, hold me near,
Times when I am down.
You'll make my day, ease my way,
This love where love is found.

Please be my friend, something you'll spend,
We will grow each passing day,
Though I am a bear, I'll always share,
I'm never that far away.

It's the trees that make me wheeze,
The climate I can hardly bear.
All those leaves, they make me sneeze,
The north, there is none there.

As the cold, the wind that blows,
The cold I cannot bear.
I search for heat, a warm retreat,
The love, I'll find it there.

I search for home, I'm not alone,
My owner he is as well.
I've not much time, you'll change your mind,
You will, she can, that's swell!

A MOMENT WITH NATE, FOR MATTY

My name is Nate, but there is a debate.
I must have faith; I'm in a slobby state.
My favourite camera is lost, an expensive cost.
It's all for naught; where it is, I forgot.
I am not too great, a saddened state.
I don't feel so great, I'm in a debate.
I have many friends who help me to no ends.
Francis, she spends; we're special friends.
Francis, she is so cool; I feel like a fool.
We go to the same school, follow the golden rule.
Nate feels lost, as the camera is lost.
Is this all for naught; soon the lines are crossed.
Nate's locker is a mess, in a state of duress.
He always feels stressed and saddened no less.
He says it's not fair; it's inside somewhere.
I left it in there; life is so unfair.
I can't take a shot; the yearbook is all for naught.
I cannot really stop; for once I was on top.
I feel so let down; my smile is upside down.
Endlessly, I walk around; I feel let down.
Teddy is my best friend; times are fun that we spend.
His math skills he defends; he is a great friend.
My friend Teddy is cool; he has just one rule.
He is a jokester, a fool; I am picked on in school.
He plays pearly whites, while the keyboard ignites.
His band is tight; The Mollusks are out of sight.
He makes me laugh; his jokes are bad.
The love of math; this I cannot grasp.
Teddy had a special name; it's uniquely strange.

I had to refrain, the square root not the same.
He hates the heights; it's a terrible sight.
The school's roof height, so high, what a fright.
Spanish, he speaks; another language is so neat.
Two ways he speaks; he's ahead of the streak.
Here is a corny joke; I hope a thought invokes.

MR. TURTLE

Perhaps the dawn, the day arose,
Sun peeked through the clouds.
The smell of summer was in the air,
Distant voices grew aloud.

Cyclists, we were eager to view,
The route we chose to ride.
Along the road and scenic trails,
Where nature seemed to hide.

With many miles, the day was long,
The path which we chose.
Along the road, nature had appeared,
Mr. Turtle, his presence arose.

A vast expanse, its width so broad,
To reach the other side.
In hopes he would not fail,
Vehicles that sped on by.

Mr. Turtle had his pride,
Trucks that roared, winds that blew.
For God was on his side,
The edge was close, in that he knew.

His hopes, dreams, plans he made,
A future was his to find.
Inching closer, no danger in sight,
He had left the past behind.

A foot or two, he was so close,
The end was now in sight.
The rains that fell, the puddle grew,
To finish it was his right.

With his hopes, they did not change,
As cyclists, we took great care.
We passed him by, without a scratch,
But for Hilda, he wasn't spared!

The wheel in front she did avoid,
The back rode straight on through.
In the end, his life was gushed,
What hit him, he never knew.

Through his back, a tire had run,
Thoughts they were so brief.
Nature's path, the road was paved,
Mr. Turtle was Hilda's grief.

As for Hilda, the speed had killed,
The little turtle, his plight doomed.
A life so short, then he died,
It darkened Hilda's gloom.

Mr. Turtle, not five inches 'round,
Eleven cyclists did evade.
As for one saddened, she was,
Mr. Turtle for now we pray.

RHYS: ENTHUSIASTIC AND CONFIDENT

There is a voice that comes to mind,
A little voice gets louder over time.
A sense of pride, not often shared,
To look inside, and Rhys is there.
To express in words a sense of pride,
For he will choose, he will decide.
Not three feet tall, he towers over us,
The spirit he carries, he never gives up.
In ways Rhys speaks to create in rhyme,
Embellished in words, created over time.
Though deep inside, his mind creates,
In words and phrases, they're great debates.
Just a year ago, an inquisitive thought,
Words he phrased; a moment had brought.
For I do not want to be just four,
Closer to death, seemed to be a chore.
The voice that rose, a sense of pride,
In his mind was a decision, he'd decide.
For five years old and far from death,
Words of reason, Rhys gained respect.
Summer had arrived, the end of class,
Months online and two months to relax.
The dock was in and summer break,
The first one to dive in the lake.
A point to process in meaning perhaps,
To challenge oneself and never go back.
To see Matty jump off the dock,
The courage and perseverance wouldn't stop.

The water rose high and from the sand,
Still over his head, a challenge at hand.
A means to float, a lifejacket donned,
A chance to swim, courage spawned.
The dock arose above the waves,
Whitecaps churned and Rhys was afraid.
And up the ladder, Matty would arrive,
Soaked to the skin, yet he survived.
One by one, each day Rhys watched,
Matty would jump, he didn't stop.
A week went by, he pondered aloud,
How to overcome, and Mommy would be proud.
Down one step, each day he tried,
Closer to the feeling stirring inside.
One by one, he was closer still,
Courage and perseverance took over his will.
Something within, a sense of pride,
For within one boy Rhys would decide.
A leap of faith to overcome,
To jump for joy, happiness for just one.
Rhys just one, the voice that speaks,
A challenge to express, encouragement he seeks.
To look for advice, in choices to decide,
Matthew, an older brother, a sense of pride.
The winds blew cold, the bay would rise,
Wavy days would come and rise so high.
To don a vest and ride the waves,
Jump for joy on a summer's day.
Summer has gone, the autumn left,
The winds blew cold and no regrets.
For winter has arrived, the snow fell,
The silence arrived, it's quiet for a spell.

The snows did fall and a wall of white,
To build a fort and a snowball fight.
To roll in the snow and disappear,
To wait and wonder for Daddy to appear.

SOFIJA: THE PRINCESS

There is a voice, chosen by choice,
A sound so familiar to seek.
Her words express, her joy no less,
To listen, what a joyous retreat.
Sofija stands so tall, not two feet tall,
She commands an audience each day.
A stroll in the park, playful she embarks,
Happiness with each passing day.
Words she speaks, pure elegance she repeats,
Her decision was not lightly made.
Her focus was chosen, the direction now frozen,
To follow her is the only way.
With hat in place and glasses placed,
Her wardrobe is now complete.
Pink coat and shoes, her stylish moves,
Her direction for now she seeks.
Upon the chair, she waits and stares,
Another night has come.
Tomorrow, a new day, a chance to play,
Excitement for everyone.
A girl on the town, to stroll around,
With uncle Jordan, this is a treat.
Sights and sounds, Toronto city grounds,
With Sam makes this day complete.
Stylish shades she wears, in disguise she shares,
The fashion industry is on fire.
A girl about town, as photographers surround,
The look is every mom's desire.

That moment Sofija stares, thinking she's aware,
Dark eyes pierce through your heart.
Within the sweet smile, knowing all the while,
Sharing this is just a little part.

WIDE-EYED AND SMILES

For one so small, eager to follow,
To search and not always find;
To explore and see, to hold and be,
To treasure for all time.

A vision in sight, smiles in delight,
Something not seen before;
A look of surprise before his eyes,
And so eager to learn more.

To point and see something he sees,
Tiptoe up and be near;
To whisper so soft, as if not to talk,
To be close and not too near.

Questions he asks, thoughts he grasps,
Pictures within his mind;
Ideas are drawn, understanding belongs,
A meaning perceived in time.

THE ELUSIVE HIDDEN CREEK

Into the woods for junk left behind,
The creek, that elusive place;
Many days ago, the trash heap flowed,
Lost in an undiscovered space.
We walked down the path, and no way back,
The light shone down from above;
The trash we collected, sorted, and inspected,
Neglected, and just tossed because.
Bags and a mask, for the smell you'd gasp,
All sorts of garbage galore;
Though we set a pace, clearing each space,
Land, where no one had come before.
With gloves and rakes, this garbage, a disgrace,
Old bottles, cans, and glass;
Each bag was weighed, the pile was displayed,
A good job was all we asked.
Together we walked, to investigate, we thought,
The creek where it ebbed and flowed;
We walked on the trail, this path would avail,
Searching for the creek, water flowed.
We passed the park, just before dark,
And down the hill to the pond;
Over the trail, Sophie would not fail,
She looked through the forest and beyond.
We strolled the path, over the stream and back,
The creek was nowhere to be found;
Darkness set in, the morning we'd begin,
The answer would soon be found.
A question was asked, a neighbour perhaps,

Natalie, an answer to our plight;
With skill and grace, Sophie began the race,
By the school, the journey was in sight.
Across the road, the adventure would unfold,
Through the trees and thick thorny brush;
Down the slope, danger invoked,
To the bottom to find what Ava believed.

CHAPTER 14
INTO THE DEEP
───────────

295 FEET; SCUBA DIVING

Beyond the blackness, beyond the depth,
Where experience rules, life gains respect;
Within the darkness, there is less light,
The struggle within, the will to fight.
Within four souls, there is a place unknown,
Trapped in the darkness, so far from home;
In a single breath, a second or less,
The terror now dwells unto the depths.
For down below Georgian Bay's floor,
Shrouded in darkness, the mystery's explored;
Yet buried inside, a world unknown,
The seas that hide, respects now grown.
Unto this darkness, a ship lies ahead,
Shrouded in darkness, the ropes now lead;
And in the void, there lies a past,
Through hundreds of years and now to grasp.
Though closer still and proudly it stands,
Lost in the distance upon foreign lands;
For in their midst, the darkness at depth,
These souls now peruse an uncertain death.
For now, what is found, a ship lies below,
These daring ones risk lives and souls;
Precious minutes, for everything can go wrong,
Still, they dare where the venture belongs.
With one wrong move is certain death,
The sport now gains all its respects;
What was found, now known to us all,
There is one risk, to risk it all.
For what was found, a way and a means,

There is no easy solution, no easy scene;
Open the box, for now it is seen,
For what's inside, light has never been.
There is no exit, no real escape,
Destined to darkness is tempting fate.
Now lies the problem, within one true way,
What is to be done, what do you say?
Beyond the depth, the challenge is the same,
The depth she lays at, 295 feet, she remains.

A WORLD OF ITS OWN

Cold and desolate is this place,
There is no one I can face.
There is no light, no means of heat,
There is no place I can retreat.
I close my eyes and pray for hope,
When I wake, the pain invokes.
I feel inside, there's no way out,
I look for answers, I'm lost in doubt.
There is no sun, no place to rest,
I do what's expected, with little respect.
I look for signs, to free what is,
I look no more, I am destined to live.
For many years, I have lived for today,
I know no other, I've lost my way.
Is there a sign, a means to free?
I'd give my life to end the siege.
I close my eyes and pray for death,
I know no more and expect no less.

A GALE IN NOVEMBER; THE *EDMUND FITZGERALD*

A day in November, on the tenth, it was said,
The last voyage of the year, the newspaper read.
A culmination of storms arrived that day,
Thrashing the Fitzgerald, twisting, bending away.
Wind, rain, sleet, snow, and hail,
The ship carried on closer to no avail.
The voice on the radio, the last word known,
We are okay and holding our own.
All 749-foot length, in a 540-foot lake depth,
The Fitzgerald was lost, all hands we respect.
Within the darkness and shattered dreams,
Yet buried beneath, through haunting scenes.
Through the windows, distorted and worn,
Now a changed history, the seas forewarned.
Within the depth, hundreds of feet below,
Some who regret where lost sailors go.
Unto the cold, a last gasp of breath,
The story is told, they paid their respects.
Through the windows, lost in the shroud,
The lives of the men whose dream disallowed.
Unto the lake, their lives had changed,
Until this day, it was never the same.
One day each year, they come to call,
They come to remember, they come to recall.
The lives of so many, for now have changed,
Remembering the dead, for here they remain.
For on that night, what happened back when,
The lake had turned, forsaking the men.

Unto this day, below the murky depths,
So little is known, lost, they struggle to forget.
Unto the darkness, lost in the depths,
The answers still lie, for now here they rest.

FAR BELOW

Far below, in the depth of man,
We voyage into foreign lands.
A hidden truth, a way of life,
Other worlds, the struggle to fight.
Far below, where tiny light lies,
Under water, in darkness, new life thrives.
Within these depths and foreign lands,
Out of touch, by the force of man.
Farther below, in the darkened depths,
So few have been and fewer regrets.
In this space, so far and few,
So many know, an insufficient few.
From time to time, a visitor is new,
The world of man, an unwilling crew.
The lives and outcasts, these ones depart,
The wreckage and rubble, an alarming part.
The struggle for life, the dominant few,
The objects above come crashing through.
They litter the floor, the bottom is disturbed,
A loss to little, so great are the words.
There will come a time, a time but soon,
The lack of space, destined and doomed.
This life so precious, they don't forsake,
The lives so few, their final mistake ...

HELLO

There was one dive, this I made,
Unto the depth, history, I'd say.
There was a problem or two,
A friend I met, a costly one too!

Unto the darkness, unto the deep,
Unto the blackness, marine life creeps.
With suit in hand, equipment to don,
Checking the regulators, then okay, I moved on.

The light soon faded, into the darkness I fell,
A foot, a second, the time took a spell.
Minutes later, the bottom I had touched,
The small shelf, the edge, was not much.

Minding my business, taking a picture or two,
The shipwreck I found; the plaque had not moved.
As for the depth, 295 feet to be exact,
A memory, a challenge, a picture to bring back.

Balanced on the edge, the focus was real,
Just to take a picture, a thump I did feel.
I met a fish, or he met me,
He scared the life out of me.

How to describe, what did I see?
For this large fish, you would kindly agree.
He was big and green, ugly, and mean,
He was long and grey, an ugly scene.

A siscowet he was, I was not prepared,
My balance lost, the camera went over there.
The strap was tethered unto my wrist,
The lanyard broke; I was pissed!

A little step was all I had made,
Into the blackness, the camera went away.
The flash went off, but it was too late,
Into the unknown, a costly mistake.

Down it fell, and down some more,
Down ever farther, onto the floor.
At the bottom, for here, to my surprise,
Now busted and broken, now here it lies.

Now at the bottom, just one hundred feet or so,
Not even intact, in the deathly cold.
As the housing just lay on the ground,
I gave it a shake and it rattled around.

I thought for a moment, it could not be,
I shook it again, busted, gee.
Remembering back when, though I was told,
It was pressured to a depth one thousand feet or so.

As my dive came to a halt,
The camera was in trouble, it was not my fault.
No wrong was done, he invaded my space,
All that I had, a memory in its place.

What should I say, what should I do?
The camera won't work, a damn pity too.
I came to the surface, I called once again,
I called once more, I waited just then.

The lights went out, alone in the dark,
Now no one around, my thoughts embarked.
I waited, and waited, then waited some more,
I waited for a voice; this was a chore.

The minutes passed, the air was now low,
I gazed at my gauge, just five minutes or so.
I waited and watched, wondered and prayed,
The darkness, the deep, the depth was grave.

All that I had hoped, all that I feared,
A light that I had, the inner voice cheered.
Hope was gone, the signs were slim,
A voice appeared, a little weak and thin.

For that moment, all went black,
Minutes passed, no way back.
As I rose, thoughts began,
Was this an accident or was it planned?

A sigh of relief when the surface was clear,
To respect the depth and warmth up here.
As for the camera, it was insured,
An absence of voice and less of words.
A voice did speak, how did it break?
I raised my hands, an honest mistake.

INTO THE DEEP

Many feet below,
Few people go,
Places where there is no light.
Into the dark,
Do they embark,
With a flashlight to find insight.
A rope leads a way,
A place to wade,
A voyage into the past.
A chance to go,
A place below,
There's no looking back.

Another time and place,
A void of space,
Down into the unknown below.
As sunlight fades,
To find a way,
To the bottom who will know.

Into this space,
An unknown place,
A world unlike our own.
Where all can breathe,
Where all are free,
A place far from our home.

Into the night,
Beyond the light,
Where sunlight never goes.
Beyond their sight,
The will to fight,
Survival of friends and foes.

MURPHY'S LAW OF SCUBA DIVING

One did say no time to get away,
Laws with no reason to be.
One wishing to dive, hoping to survive,
Explanations one seemingly doesn't see.

Though all seems well, though hard to tell,
The journey has just begun.
With smooth and ease, just a breeze,
Too simple and complex to some.

Some who pursue and are willing to do,
At times it doesn't go right.
What goes wrong will go wrong,
In the end, it's just not right.

Though left alone, soon full blown,
From bad to worse, you'll see.
Easy at first, changing for worse,
Never smooth as a breeze.

It doesn't seem right, the will to fight,
To change is just a fool.
No chance to change or rearrange,
Never to change is the rule.

To change its course will do most force,
Wrong is still and will be.
The damage it does, reasons because,
That's the way it would be.

Nature, it rules, at times it's cruel,
Fairness is not a part.
Hidden within, changes begin,
With treasures hidden in the dark.

Though all seems well, times you can tell,
Something mustn't be right.
What went wrong, what doesn't belong,
Boggling the mind who is right?

Murphy's law to dive, still survive,
Whatever may go wrong.
Think absolute, don't be a goof,
Stop, think, and be strong.

OUTSIDE LOOKING IN

A world of wonder,
A place hidden under,
A place where all can see.
Its beauty beneath,
Where marine life breathes,
A place where all are free.

A world inside,
Where all can hide,
In secret passages below.
With spectacular colours,
Hundreds of feet under,
Brilliance for all to know.

Its beauty below,
For all who know,
Wondrous things to see.
The ocean's alive,
Where all things thrive,
Where the warm seas flow.

Beneath a sea of blue,
In oceans hold true,
At times hidden to our eyes.
One must look closely,
To discover the most,
There are treasures inside.

There's another place,
Beyond this space,
A place only known by some.
So they travel down under,
To a place of wonder,
A challenge discovered by everyone.

A world is alive,
Though many secrets hide,
Where miles of ocean abound.
What lies ahead,
Words have yet be said,
New discoveries can be found.

In the depths below,
Where few who venture go,
Beneath the ocean floor.
Pieces of the past,
A time long past,
Discoveries open new doors.

Below the rich blue water,
Descended by our fathers,
Into a place long ago.
Discoveries of the seas,
Pieces of history,
Buried many years ago.

*A sense of wonder,
The place to discover,
How it came to be.
Untouched by man,
Beneath the shifting sand,
Buried for a century.*

*Now undisturbed,
Man has preserved,
Pieces of time long gone.
He's taken away,
Preciously saved,
What he did, was it wrong?*

QUESTIONS OF THE DEEP

Ships abound, ships are found,
Hidden on the floor beneath.
Archaeologists find lost over time,
Vessels lost on the reefs.

Under the coves, where no one goes,
Down into the depths so deep.
In waters so cold, few are so bold,
Where in the water are creatures beneath?

In search of ways, of past many days,
Where many vessels once sailed.
Pieces of time, lost over time,
Mysteries in sea shanty tales.

Those who explored, searching for more,
With the knowledge to understand.
Why they came, how life changed,
To journey to other lands.

Parts of history, buried at sea,
Nestled in the cargo hold.
In the darkened seas, few will ever see,
Where few who venture to go.

Tanks with air, some who dare,
To go beyond the limit.
To learn as they dive and will to survive,
To experience life in it.

Beyond the grasp to seek this task,
Many feet down, some will go.
The will to explore, to open the door,
Who knows how far just to know?

To light the way, to search today,
To study history long gone.
Searching for clues, in artifacts they used,
With the will to venture on.

Some who yearn, willing to learn,
How cultures lived here before.
To take a hold, an artifact of old,
The knowledge to discover more.

A thousand breaths, to unknown depths,
A place where some can breathe.
A way and means to find the dreams,
A time just to be free.

Few have seen, more have dreamed,
How we are capable to breathe.
To move with ease, about the seas,
How can one feel so free?

To learn and cope, to gauge and scope,
To discover what is down there.
To gaze and see, to search reality,
History, a discovery to share.

THE SPACE WITHIN DIVING

Void of life,
Yet destined despite.
For all that lives down there.
Upon the depths,
There is no less,
No lights in the darkness, beware.

Beyond the depth,
We're visitors, no less,
To a space within our time.
As we venture below,
So little we know,
Within the answers we'll find.

Unto the dark,
These souls embark,
With light we see our way.
The shadows that cast,
To guide our path,
Yet destined to venture a way.

The hours it seems,
The darkness has been,
The lives that thrive below here.
Deep in these depths,
Their lives, no less,
So little of life seems to appear.

For hours it seems,
The bottom is not seen,
The floor, it hasn't been seen.
Above what lies,
A darkened disguise,
Lifeless and destined, we've seen.

As for sea life,
That moves into our sight,
The light that blinds their way.
A sudden knock,
Their plight stops,
Our presence obstructed their way.

CHAPTER 15
PEOPLE

A GIFT REVEALED MANY YEARS TO ACQUIRE

At times, she is silent, yet so unaware,
Perhaps a mystery, unable to share.
And yet a spark, she's filled with life,
And still a vision, the adventure delights.
With Emily's smile, the warmth is there,
Perhaps distant, alluring, and fair.
Perhaps her voice, a softness set apart,
Yet unaware, a new beginning, a start.
And the mystery not often shared,
There's something hidden beyond out there.
Within her voice, an aspect of life,
Her will being one and so few dislikes.
For, as the days, Emily's adventure begins,
A challenge is met, a challenge from within.
Perhaps one day, this side will be revealed,
Now lost in the moment, the secret is concealed
As for your gift, it's cherished within,
As for the joy, this life begins.
The vision, an idea, so begins the change,
The focus to reveal, to interpret remains.
Upon each line, another to voice,
A character to reveal, with grace and poise.
To view, to gauge, to instruct, to express,
To reveal the scene and try one's best.
To search for reasons, the ability to forsake,
To capture the moment none can replace.
To hold the audience and make them a part,
To mould and inspire, to share from your heart.

CHRIS GODDARD "SILVERGHOST"

A GAME OF GOLF; THE HAZARDS OF OLD AGE

The day had dawned, the sun shone bright,
A voice did call, in sheer delight.
A game of golf, or so he said,
Ugh!! That feeling, this, I would dread.

A sprinkle of rain, the night before,
The course to see, was soggy and more.
We donned our shoes and walked to greet,
A day of golf, oh, what a treat.

Two months to the day, for John had retired,
Few aches and pains, flexibility he had acquired.
Upon the greens, his confidence stirred,
A beautiful shot was mumbled in his words.

Upon the green, the ball was placed,
Upon the tee, would mark his place.
He motioned to stretch, to creak and moan,
These sounds I heard, even a groan.

The club was chosen, a glove now placed,
He winced and stared, in a distant space.
To focus and watch, to wait my turn,
The swing perhaps, this was a concern.

The swing was chosen, the final decree,
A whack of the club, the ball was free.
It flew and travelled so far,
It came to rest, John would make par.

The shot travelled, high in the air,
This tree was placed, it did not fare.
The impact was blunt, the tree survived,
I hope it's there next time I arrive.

The chip, perhaps, did not fare well,
Over the green, goodbye for a spell.
One putt, two putts, three putts, a dream,
The first hole, nine or ten it seems.

Many shots he did try, to find the green,
Try as he may, was not as it seems.
The water was dark, swift-moving too,
Many balls were lost, this was so true.

For many shots, some high and low,
Some found the green, some we will never know.
A game of golf and day of fun,
A game, a sport, not for everyone.

To curse and swear, to laugh and cry,
To explore the outdoors, one chance to try.
To lose a ball, just hit one more,
A day of fun, who's keeping score?

By the eighteenth hole, John found his groove,
To strike the ball, he could not lose.
The ting from a club, into the air,
To find the green, just beyond, out there.

A moment to ponder, a moment or two,
Time just to think, what is the next move?
A ball so close to John's surprise,
Missed him by inches, as it flew on by.

An inch left, or to the right,
This might have ended his will to fight.
A word was spoken, to my sensitive ears,
This word perhaps some should not hear.

The final putt and some time to voice,
To express his concern and God-given choice.
And sense of ease and apology spoken,
A kind-hearted word, a gesturally token.

A day of golf in the great outdoors,
We don our masks, to breathe a chore.
The sun is bright, and friends are near,
Hurray for retirement, it is finally here.

A NUN ABOVE US ALL; A VERY HABITABLE CHARACTER

There is a driving force that steers her course,
Her spirit is infectious to all.
She is a guiding choice, a calming voice,
Heavenly, she surpasses us all.
A gentle heart, caring, is one a part,
A nun above us all.
The cross she bears, each day she wears,
A guiding light that cannot fall.
As we travel through time, a snapshot in mind,
Moments many of us now share.
As we gather 'round, our deep friendships found,
Perhaps now, we grin and bear.
A soft-spoken voice, a God-given choice,
A calming presence to us all.
She commands, with respect and grace you'd expect,
Praying for us one and all.
A challenge to heed, and so she believes,
Each task at hand to seek.
A hero to all, towering above us all,
To compare, you will not compete.
A moment to ponder, a while longer,
In places, faces of the past.
A snapshot in mind, in younger times,
We hope our friendship will surpass.
Friends who gather 'round, memories are found,
In forty short years are revealed.
Many trips were taken, photos now forsaken,

In the moment I am about to reveal.
Joanie found one place, in a heavenly space,
High above the calming seas.
Parasailing perhaps, her judgment no lapse,
A vision, high above the breeze.
A time once taken, and not forsaken,
To travel up, a treacherous road.
The sheer cliff drops, she dares not stop,
The view was worth it, you know.
Her ability to move, a vintage groove,
Dancing is a heavenly gift.
Hips in the air, motions with great flair,
She can give us all a lift.
The music did arise, to the heaven and sky,
To partake in one last dance.
A question was asked, one time, our last,
Nor shy was Joanie's subtle glance.
The lady in red, or so it was said,
The wine, this was not spared.
To hold her close, in a somber pose,
With grace, a memory now shared.
In words and songs, with grace she belonged,
A voice, her voice, is heavenly praised.
Many days and nights, aided her plight,
An angel in her formidable ways.
Though back in the day, her black-and-white ways,
A chance to strut her stuff.
A sister act, an inhabitable cast,
To dance and sing was just luck.

Behind closed doors, a screen was exposed,
She listens with great intent.
To discuss in detail, and to never fail,
Her wisdom was always heaven sent.
A question was asked, a secretive task,
An eightieth birthday wish to declare.
A chance to pose, and with no clothes,
In a birthday suit, twelve would bare.
A year in review, so what can we do,
Many places we used to go.
We wear a disguise, our faces we hide,
Please let this COVID-19 go.

A SPLASH OF LIFE

Upon the land, a gentle rain,
A sparking of life dawned remained.
Upon the rocks, the rain that fell,
Slippery, at best, dampened spirits as well.

Yet the cold now mixed with rain,
Unto this day had changed.
These lifeless souls within this time,
Observing the weather changed our minds.

One daring soul tried in vain,
Eager to fish, unbothered by the rain.
On the rocks and to his feet,
A mission, an act, a means to greet.

The rain that fell, the rocks did shine,
A feat to conquer, stumbling at times.
An hour passed, no fish in sight,
No sun to warm, no means to fight.

A loss of spirit, an effort entailed,
No strikes to see a mission failed.
Another soul, a voice did call,
For here I am and beware all.

One voice did call, slippery when wet,
The rocks are smooth, caution, better yet.
Assuring the mind, an answer replied,
Slowly he graced, slippery he realized.

Down came the rain and blackened sky,
Down deep no fish, determined to try.
A sudden pause, no voice to hear,
No sound arose, was Bill still here?

Suddenly a sound, a shuffling of feet,
Then a splash unto the deep.
A giggle, turned to laughter and a cry,
All went silent, and so did I.

I walked steadily onto the rocks I knew,
My eyes had seen a moment or two.
The water was cool, downright cold!
Summer was here, it didn't seem so.

Into the water, an unlucky one too,
Stumbling yet stunned, a moment he knew.
Unto his feet and well-soaked through,
Humbling by the fire and a warming brew.

A picture or two, a moment to decide,
A photo to remember, a place to dry.
Warmth of the fire, clothes were placed,
A time for warming, a happier state.

At this moment, we're seemingly unaware,
Clothes drying close to the fire dared.
Minutes passed, soon sizzling, almost dry,
Smoldering, then a blaze, a last goodbye.

The camera now captured a moment in time,
The film to be developed would shine.
Unto this day, these souls would rise,
The beginning of summer, they survived.

EARL OF GREY

Once I read and read some more,
For what I'd found 'twas a chore.
With these words, this meaning is found,
And so complex, ye olden town.
Alas, 'tis true, these words do rhyme,
They flowed with ease, the English kind.
For as the thought yet so diverse,
My will to try and so converse.
Mark through yonder, for 'tis, alas,
A fair young maiden for this perhaps.
Her skin so soft, warm to the touch,
Hear me now, this means so much.
For sleight of hand and warming thought,
Alas, this flower, for I have brought.
Perhaps its beauty and love are found,
Hath plucked its life no longer 'round.
For this I bring, alas, you'll see,
The Earl of green hath handcuffed me.
For on this block, my head is placed,
No longer to see, God bless my fate.
Perhaps the dungeon is better still,
To ease away thine broken will.
If you pass this way you'll come,
My fair young maiden, this lovely one.

FAIR MAIDEN

Alas, fair maiden, and so it's true,
This thing for which I've found.
This a feeling known all too well,
It grows when you are around.

With these days, they are so long,
The hours grow longer still.
When we meet, this time again,
Will ease my broken will.

There is a smile that reappears,
The moment when you are around.
Then a laugh, a sign resides,
The cold is no longer found.

Now I ponder this time away,
Perhaps a moment or two.
With this feeling to steal a kiss,
To know there are so few.

In this moment, in that I share,
I know our time is few.
Alas, fair maiden, I bid you farewell,
This love I cannot lose.

When I am alone, the cold resides,
The love that I have lost.
So I remember my time today,
Our paths for when next we cross.

MAID MARIAN

The days of yore, ye olden kind,
To find my way yet lost sometime.
To speak of truth has got my tongue,
These words I used, I speak with for one.
Alas, 'tis true, these words do rhyme,
They flowed with ease, the English kind.
What distance beyond the castle stood there?
Over the hills, trees, my venture fared.
Upon this steed, to venture away.
To wend through trees, I mark each day.
The vicious beasts that lurk nearby,
The mighty sword is by my side.
Has the sun thou brightly shined,
To squint and search, yet far I find.
These maps of cloth, rain doth fade,
The distance I seek, yet far away.
Each mile I travel, yet farther I seek,
Each passing day, my heart still weeps.
Upon the dusk, these creatures dwell,
I rest for now to cast a spell.
For as the thought yet so diverse,
My will to try and so converse.
Alas, dear maiden, for your love seeks,
To avenge your honour, in this I speak.
Skin so soft, the warmth you share,
Hear me now, for a love so fair.
Mark through yonder, for 'tis alas,
A fair young maiden for this perhaps.
Alas these flowers, for I have brought,

Your beauty yet found compares and not.
Perhaps its beauty and love are found,
Hath plucked its life no longer 'round.
For this I bring, alas, you will see,
This special feeling inside of me.
To find the castle just over the rise,
The tower is lit to my surprise.
Yet in the room, the light does appear,
Riding up to the gate, still guarded here.
Over the bridge, up to the door,
To announce to all, your knight is here.

MAIDEN JOURNEY

*Alas, fair maiden, I'm in distress,
I've lost my way and I'm under duress.
Into the forest, this place I've found,
To be alone, this sadness is 'round.*

*Many days and nights, still I believe,
A moment sometime, and still I grieve.
Alone in the dark, I wonder still,
To see you there, ease my will.*

*For in the tower, alone you wait,
Marked with time, until we mate.
Across the land and over the hills,
I ride to meet you, a moment still.*

*All the while, alone in space,
A dragon appeared and marked my fate.
With sword in hand, the fight goes on,
My will to ease before I'm gone.*

*A fiery breath and heart a-fire,
Struggling to win, to extinguish my desire.
My heart is warm and will is strong,
By your side is where I belong.*

*Through the night and all next day,
The challenge to defeat and ride away.
Yet bruised and bleeding and muscles sore,
I defeat this foe and just one more.*

Into the night, and still I ride,
Unto the dawn, soon by your side.
A man I met on my journey home,
Has joined the ranks to a place unknown.

He speaks in tongues, for which I'm lost,
Words are foreign, at times get crossed.
I think he's French and speaks too fast,
I'm unable to response that fast.

When I return, a lesson or two,
May ease my will, this tongue so true.

HANGRY THROUGH THE CHANGE'S NEW INSIGHT

So you begin to accept the change,
For life is hard, it's never the same.
You look to the future, what lies ahead,
With your head up high, you look ahead.
With the courage and grace of a man,
You'll make it back, I know you can.
From where you've come, the changes within,
And so the journey from where it begins.
Upon each step, so many you'll take,
You'll never look back and never forsake.
With new direction, upon a new path,
A brighter future, a promise you'll be back.
From the dawn, we build new hopes,
As for today, somehow you'll cope.
For the future, it has its ways,
A new beginning, as a brighter day.
Perhaps, as time when things get tight,
Like falling apart, a change in mid-flight.
With the seeds, so begins a change,
In the garden, the soul regains.
Upon the flower grows big and strong,
With the love, the caring belongs.
Each day you'll learn and strive for more,
You can endure, that's what love is for.
For all your values, it's more than friends,
As for our time, indeed, this will lend.
As each day, you'll learn and grow,
Deep inside, the memories will flow.

With these friends and every goodbye,
A chance for changes will soon be realized.
Dear friend of mine, and for your thoughts,
A few I've added, a moment that you've brought.
Perhaps this day, it will be the last,
As the memories, forever in my grasp.
And with a smile, the sadness within,
So begins my task, the sharing now begins.

HUMBLED TO THE CORE; JUST KIND OF IN LIMBO

Those of us who are aware,
Waiting and wondering to share,
Getting a booster shot, only when?
As our patience, we wait,
The answer in haste!
How long this time do we spend.
We strive to keep calm,
Just moving forward and beyond,
Still sixty-plus years we wait.
With two shots received,
Six months in we believe,
Just one more booster is our debate.
Waiting a hundred-and-sixty-eight days to receive,
A third dose, we believe,
To finally be immunized, for what next?
Most who are sixty-eight and beyond,
Inside, for our immunity, we are strong,
Now we wait silently to expect.
Giving thanks we pray,
For each and every day,
To be double vaccinated for now!
Some who cannot receive,
Awaiting, they still believe,
Thankful we have had our two.
The hours she spends,
Calling to no ends,
Looking for the answer that would suffice!
The days passed her by,

But one individual realized,
This story worthy would make it all right!
A biology teacher by trade,
Understanding the human body's ways,
Discovering the immune system traits.
The evolution of life,
The anatomy and strife,
Knowledge for the vaccine these awaits.
We have a celebrity in our midst,
Though her shyness persists,
The newspaper journalist disagrees.
As the Toronto Star wrote,
Creating an article as she spoke,
Just being in a limbo, she agrees.
We are honoured by a unique soul,
Who has taken great control,
Humbled by all she has done.
One who would never call,
Who is cared for by us all,
She is special, with gratitude from everyone!

SIDEKICKS

There was a notion, concoction, and potion,
An idea that came to light.
To choose a side, willingness to try,
Existence, a challenge despite.
No rhyme or reason, or time of season,
To achieve this task at hand.
A moment to grasp, the cash at last,
The expense required a plan.
Buried just beneath, the overwhelming heap,
Packages David now savoured he'd try.
The decision, perhaps, which one to grasp,
To toss a coin to decide.
Too numerous to count, this endless amount,
Of facts, figures, calories to consume.
For in the end, a chance to spend,
Quality time, creating more room.
Within the room, square feet now doomed,
Each box this space did acquire.
Stacked to the roof, invasion consumed,
Less space, less talking would inspire.
A chance to grasp, a moment at last,
Now all seems black and white.
A moment to ponder, a little while longer,
So begins the endless fight.
A moment to grasp, to hold back the laughs,
Create a meal with inspiration longer.
The enjoyment of sides, kick up your pride,
Emptiness and space will take a while longer.

TANKS, BUDDY; SOMETHING YOU 'MEMBER PRETTY GOOD

I think of Mom when I think of these words,
Others who think I might be disturbed.
For these sayings, some are just words,
Part of my past and a little diverse.
Mom always said I must do the dishes,
These chores of mine had good wishes.
The cloth I used, yet strange to some,
The cup towel, the word has become.
Then mopping the floor, a duty fulfilled,
The workings involved a technical skill.
The floor in part and trim, indeed,
Called the mop board, we all agreed.
Making a bed, a task in itself,
All those covers, the warmth is always felt.
The comforter of sorts but it's not the same,
For this the puff, yet similar by name.
The word to describe, it is that thing,
Though what to call it is something that rings.
Something that works, that does good,
Just something, a word, you think is pretty good.
Across the land, especially down home,
He's a friend of mine, something I own.
He lives next door, he's seen in the street,
This buddy of mine, he's neat.
A word to describe something to say,
Gesundheit bless you, tanks, anyways.
Yet a problem you have, something out there,
You got to 'member, it all seems fair.

Perhaps just a sport, to some so boring,
They call them wrestlers trapped in a ring.
Times they've been there, somewhere out there's,
A place I know well, 'member down there.
But most of all, the food of feasts,
Mouth-watering meals, perhaps not least.
Cabbage and corn, veggies most of all,
Them boiled dinners, my buddies, us all.
My place down home, I 'member most of all,
Many tanks to 'member, my buddies, them all.
Anywhere you'd find them jumping just a lot,
More than stickers, them all I got.

TEACHING; A LEARNING EXPERIENCE

The authority to do, knowledge to move,
To convey within a thought.
The will to survive, teaching in stride,
The goal and ability one's taught.

To know and learn, a sense of concern,
The knowledge to understand.
Time you shared, knowing you cared,
The task you take by hand.

To judge all fair, to always be aware,
To encourage when they're so young.
To mould their minds, taking the time,
Though vulnerable when they are young.

Students you reach, your ability to teach,
Through learning, all will care.
Enrich young minds, knowing in time,
The acceptance that all will share.

The voice of rule, the voice that rules,
The one who has the right.
Organize and control, the class as a whole,
Only one will choose their plight.

Strict though gentle, harsh yet subtle,
To understand, encourage, and explain.
A sense of pride, knowing you tried,
Your time is not in vain.

CHRIS GODDARD "SILVERGHOST"

The ones who know, eventually shows,
The source that all will bond.
One who divides, one who tries,
The one, the only, the strong.

The feeling within, a caring begins,
To reach out and feel.
To apply what's taught, place into thoughts,
Graduation, the diploma, is real.

THE GUTS, THE GLORY; GOLF, IT'S JUST A GAME

Upon the greens, four souls took hold,
Before us the mist, with it the cold.
Daring souls, to challenge we agreed,
A moment to grasp, a memory to believe.

Upon each club and balls in hand,
Tees now secured unto uncharted lands.
A cart to ride, four wheels in all,
No speed too fast, no terrain too small.

Perhaps the clan, two rookies, indeed,
Two rookies to aid, instructions they'd need.
Upon their feet, with clubs in hand,
Within a grip, to conquer new lands.

A swing or two, a moment to grasp,
To strike with fear, the moment at last.
As Susie waited a place upon the tee,
With nerves of steel, this moment would see.

A final prayer, the swing was praised,
The ball went a-blazing, two feet it strayed.
Now for Nancy, the second of two,
To follow the lead, this moment she knew.

With a crack, the ball was away,
And yet a tree, harbouring the way.
A lucky break, the ball had ceased,
The luck of God, a moment of peace.

Now for Bill, with game in hand,
Confident he was, this a final stand.
A weary soldier, a moment to breathe,
The ball took air and got lost in the weeds.

The next to the tee, Chris took a stand,
Ball of orange, in the distance it'd land.
Perhaps the last, a seasoned soul,
Upon the crack and there it goes.

We zigged and zagged, we drove on down,
A lesson or two, over leaps and bounds.
Upon each stroke, still closer we moved,
Perhaps the flag, the excitement grew.

Shrouded in the mist, the flag appeared,
The balls no closer, the moment was here.
Upon the green, to aim with ease,
With putter in hand, the ball disagreed.

The ball did roll, at times just beyond,
Past the hole at times, it was gone.
Obstacles we found difficult at times,
Out of the blue, patience soon shined.

Courageous we dared the obstacles we found,
Tracks, towers, trees, other wildlife around.
Instilled with confidence, with patience and ease,
The ladies had shown in themselves they'd believe.

The guys in doubt, the ladies soon found,
The cumbersome task, the distance was found.
The stroke wasn't one, or two or three,
Seven through ten, it's fun as they agreed.

The ladies' ability improved, never before,
Overshooting the men, bettering their scores.
Into the sand traps, the ball did find,
In bushes and streams, a word would find.

A curse or swear, a voice, damn ball,
A thud, splash, ting, as nature did call.
The fifteenth at last, the eighteenth still grew,
The fun we had a-striking few.

Nearer the hole, a soul did ask,
For one to move, a moment to ask.
Addressing the ball, head set down,
As a fly did grace, the club went around.

A sudden flash just missed Bill's head,
Into the bushes suddenly he fled.
Discouraged and bruised, appearing ahead,
This shot never matched, an apology was said.

With grace and poise as Bill soon neared,
Walking unhurt, his humour appeared.
Soon the eighteenth, the nineteenth neared,
Cool drinks and food, a rest persevered.

A moment to praise a final thought,
Four strong souls, the game was fought.
A day of fun, a game of golf and time,
Within each a moment, in each they shined.

THE PAR IS PART OF THE GOAL

To focus and address and gain respect,
Alignment, a crucial part to succeed.
Take aim to the green, something to be seen,
An ace sinking one in three.

An amateur, perhaps, as time will pass,
The funds should not be seen.
The approach, the skill, patience, your will.
The ball upon the green.

Away, perhaps, in time will pass,
The club you must assign.
Take aid to ease, backspin, might agree,
To check that all important line.

The caddie, your chap, the weight on his back,
The cart, the fortunate will ride.
To assign the grip, interlocking a tip,
All fingers to grasp will abide.

Your stance is closed, some might oppose,
The ones left out in the rain.
You've closed, now faced, strike the ball with haste,
To look you now must refrain.

There is an effect that one must regret,
The ability, the right to decide.
Part of the course is par on the course,
The challenge leaves the frustration aside.

The need for one to overcome,
The hills and valley and lakes.
For on the beach, some who can reach,
A sinking feeling to debate.

'TWAS THE NIGHT BEFORE AT THE LUKASIKS; A PAINTING AFFAIR

'Twas the night before at the Lukasik's, and all through the house,
Not a soul was sleeping, not even the mouse.
The drapes were undone, the hooks on display,
The sheets now hanging in disarray.
The lights were all covered, and wrapped up tight,
To prevent the fine powder from electrifying this night.
The windows all covered, no decorations were found,
With no tree in the corner, no festive things were found.
Upon the wall, the projector shone bright,
Casting shadows, as dust danced in the light.
No sounds of Christmas music, no carolers were 'round,
No "Joy to the World," just emptiness surrounds.
This year's festive events would have to wait,
Thirty years of old paint was an utter disgrace.
With goggles and gloves, and masks to conceal.
Jumpsuits of white, this now . . . felt real.
The holes were filled, and sanding began,
Now covered in white, with a fine chalky sand.
The air was thick, the dust now fine,
It clings to everything, was this a bad time?
No party to hold, no friends could we afford,
No extras to exercise, no willing bodies scored.
The ladders were erect, and all draped in white,
The array of new paint cans was such a delight.
The paint chips were hanging, all over the house,
So many colours to choose from, there was some doubt.
The floor was draped, with tarps galore,
A daunting task, who's up for the chore?

With poles and brushes and rollers and trays,
Now all lined up, in an organized way.
The windows all decorated, and taped in blue,
Hoping to avoid the long-awaited glue.
The decision now taken, what room to start,
Do we wait till the morning to do our part?
A glass of wine, to ponder and reason,
A festive choice for the upcoming season.
The can was soon opened, we awaited the surprise,
The colour was chosen, patiently before our eyes.
The minutes and hours, the days and weeks,
The final coating, and a daunting relief.
The paint now dried, and cleanup began,
We forged through the dawn, in uncharted lands.
A lesson now learned, to complete this task,
Next time we do this, the professional painters we ask.

THE MYSTIC MAN

I have seen the mystic man,
His wisdom, there are no bounds;
I believe in what he sees,
The vision is all around.

In the darkness and silence hushed,
To whisper there is no need;
As for his powers that evolve within,
It is only to believe.

Upon the table, crystal ball,
The stand that holds its place;
This sacred globe and magic within,
The mystery within is placed.

As for the cards and detailed drawings,
From within the fortunes told;
With each new card another reveals,
For the lives of others unfolds.

Within the palms, these lines are placed,
For each there lies new life;
Though the passages that intersect
Bring new understanding to light.

And through the ball, the spirits rise,
For unto this place, they seek;
Into this house, the voices speak,
Unto our lives, they creep.

As the darkness, the light appears,
For truth, there is no doubt;
As for the cards that speak of youth,
The spirit now moves about.

For as his voice that speaks to those,
The darkness moves all around;
And in the shadows that lurk within
The future, the key, is found.

THE PRIDE OF ONE; THE COACH

There's a smile upon a face,
So gentle and kind, hard to replace.
In silence, the words are not spoken,
Thoughts that are read by a simpler token.

Perhaps just for one, the deeds are vast,
Yet this one the outcomes surpassed.
As the task, the enthusiasm becomes,
Joy that it brings, the moments for some.

As the coach who instructs and guides,
As each task in one that takes pride.
Carried inside, a feeling like no other,
Shared, she shows, like a sister or brother.

Yet a smile upon a face,
Through caring and pride, a warm embrace.
As the thought, and for her time,
A spirit and team, a caring in mind.

THE HALF-CENTURY CLUB

We often wonder, the world we live under,
How will our lives have changed?
Each day we strive, one more to survive,
Will tomorrow still be the same?

Each day we go forth, we remember the fourth,
June is a month for fun.
Mimi's has become special for some,
We have arrived to celebrate just one.

The day has dawned, the struggle to move on,
This day has finally come.
For one who is close, Mimi means the most,
A birthday wishes, everyone.

You're now a member, lifelong to remember,
The half-century club you have earned.
Fifty long years of laughter and tears,
Today, this day, it is your turn.

Fifty years, what a feat, a challenge to defeat,
The next fifty, we can only hope.
To partake in math, few can only grasp,
Six-hundred-months-old is no joke.

This parade of cars, travelling from afar,
One challenge to overcome.
To coordinate and surprise, a sense of pride.
With thanks to everyone.

TOUCHDOWN IN THE ENZONE

A sense of pride before these eyes,
One challenge to overcome.
The knowledge learned, no real concerns,
Respect from one to one.

Methodical and precise, his brain a device,
Churning and thinking out loud.
A rhythmical place, delivered without haste,
A sense that he can be proud.

The morning routine, dramatically seen,
Of products too numerous to recall.
In boxes and bags, cartons, liquids aside,
Inventory, we count on it all.

Upon the throne, he feels at home,
Behind the wheel of his success.
The years have changed, he's still the same,
It's what others will expect.

Radio set loud, in sports some are proud,
Of stats who played and won.
A bet is laid, cash now paid,
Victory and the day were done.

These picks are savoured, the stats, who's favoured,
The sport, the game, a right.
Is it under or over a race till it's over?
Never to give up without a fight.

Quiet and reserved, at times not heard,
Observing the traffic at bay.
The challenge to defeat, bad drivers who lead,
Sounds the horn won't display.

There is a routine that must be seen,
To observe the skill firsthand.
Each step is rehearsed and later well-versed,
To his countless adoring fans.

The final play, just seconds away,
The ball is snapped then thrown.
Into the air, a player aware,
Touchdown in the . . . Enzone.

WOODY TINDER MCSPLINTER

I wandered in here to keep warm,
To dry my branches, rest my bones.
An exotic wood, now domesticated I fear,
This place so foreign, the dirt floor here.
A handsome fellow, a place to relax,
To sit awhile and take a nap.
Many days I have been alone in here,
I waited for someone, just to appear.
All day I wait to see one soul,
To comfort me and share my woes.
Sun shines down, my leaves of green,
The winter has passed, as spring is seen.
They water me, just once a day,
And trim my branches other days.
My hat is placed atop my head,
Hair being short, thinning I dread.
Flowers now bloom and full of life,
A happier place like birds in flight.
The people come, just for a while,
Share their thoughts, make me smile.
One day a woman approached,
And sat beside me in an overcoat.
She put her hand upon my knee,
A sudden feeling that shook this tree.
She placed her arm inside mine,
Sensational feeling at the time.
She spoke of faces and places she had been,
The stories she told turned me green.
After a while she walked away,

Brushed past me on her way.
She hesitated as she turned,
A last glance, a final word.
Goodbye, dear friend, it will be soon,
We will talk more, one day soon.
A sudden feeling of stiffness I did not know,
A sensation as the sap inside flowed.
The sun was fading, darkness soon passed,
Another day, once more she will be back.
A memory I share each passing day.
Who was that woman who sat here one day?

WOODSY MCTIMBER STALWART: MAN OF THE FOREST

Perhaps one day I will take a stroll,
Into the forest, for a friend or foe.
I followed the path, down to the stream,
To find a handsome fellow of my dreams.
He stood so lean, just twelve feet tall,
A brownish complexion yet quiet above all.
An exotic wood, to create a desire,
Don't light a match, for I might retire.
Created from a plan, each line was required,
To carve my features, good looking, I desired.
The years soon passed, my branches frayed,
Slowly dropping off, my camouflage once swayed.
I used to have hair, way up there,
And some near, the middle down here.
As the years passed, it grew,
I thought one day I'd touch the sky.
Some who come to stay awhile,
To photograph me, a selfie style.
They do not talk or question me,
They wander off, damn dogs like to pee.
I stopped to gaze into his eyes,
A moment passed, a feeling in disguise.
A branch appeared, suddenly it was stiff,
So soft and round, I couldn't resist.
A feeling of stiffness, I did not know,
A sensation as the sap inside him flowed.
A liquid flowed and down the tree,
An opaque solution, a knotty disease.

I reached over and gave him a hug,
He grabbed my behind and a little rub.
A peck on the cheek, I said my goodbyes,
Tears appeared, man of the forest, wooden inspired.

THROUGH THE LOOKING GLASS; LES ONCE MORE

A question was posed, the challenge I rose,
For is it windows that I clean?
As Les did ask, unsure I'd grasp,
The true meaning, I'm stuck in between.

I look and stare to the place out there,
A time I remember back when.
Sun set aglow, the warm winds blow,
Summer brings it back again.

The view outside, the dirty snow hides,
Windows need a cleaning soon.
With tools in hand, I have a plan,
To rid this doom and gloom.

The ladder awaits, my buck I take,
A solution I will not reveal.
With squeegee and mop, I will not stop,
Until the day that spring heals.

I have a debate, the spring I will wait,
The air way up there is thin.
The higher you climb, motionlessly at times,
Soon the uneasiness begins.

A fear of heights, acrophobia, being polite,
Ability to travel higher resides.
I will refrain, avoid the strain,
Because I have a window guy.

UNMASKING . . . THE TRUTH IS REVEALED

I can, I make, have and forsake,
The rise of everything in sight.
The size of my pension and daily tension,
How can I make it right?

Looking at the sign, from time to time,
At the slot machine, I seem to lose.
The gas prices rise, the sign never lies,
Reverting to walking, I must choose.

Lines on my face, the masking makes,
The ability to take in a breath.
My ears have creased, pain has eased,
Knowing now what to expect.

My ability to choose, the cash to lose,
The rules I've forgotten somehow.
The makeup rules, out of practice, I lose,
YouTube will make me proud.

New foundation will rise, makeup to decide,
Then the blush a warming shade.
On my lips, a choice, as my inner voice,
Colour now blended, a new day.

My eyes a liner proves and nothing to lose,
Adding makeup, a colour to decide.
Eye shadow a tone, brush and go it alone,
Crimp the lashes, the final try.

Remembering what I have lost, the final cost,
To look in the mirror and one last glance.
A chance walks, without a thought,
Change my mind, to have a chance.

Months have passed, my wits now dashed,
My world awaits, once concealed.
My list has grown, I am not alone,
Unmasking the truth now revealed.

THE WARMING EFFECT OF FOOT BAGS

It's mornings I dread, getting out of bed,
The floor is cold to the bone.
I look for a feat, a warming treat,
Keeping my poor old feet warm.

I feel a draft, below the door crack,
Cold air flows, affects us all.
That cold breeze, the warmth I need,
To stand upright or I'll fall.

A history lesson nears for five thousand years,
The ability to keep our feet in rags.
To cover our soles, protection as a whole,
Referring to them as simple foot bags.

As time marched on, technology dawned,
The knitting machine, elastic and nylon.
Who would have thought, knitting had brought?
Stockings and leggings march on.

A history moved on, fashion belonged,
Socks had a place to play.
Pockets for each toe, a place to grow,
A separation needed, a place to stay.

Changes in time, inventions, and designs,
Friends with benefits had a place.
The sections, equal spacing to stay,
Putting on nail polish has a space.

A favourite pair with a flair,
Long, short, colourful, or sheer.
Styles with shoes, sandals won't lose,
A warming effect we hold this dear.

POLY-GNOMIALS

Sitting here all by myself,
I gaze unto the sky.
Looking up at the world above,
Damn bird just flew on by.

Washed and clean, I am now a mess,
I am not a pretty sight.
Bird poop has covered me,
Once red and blue, now black and white.

Many of us grace yards and lawns,
Funny how small we seem to be.
Quizzical features we all share,
Little elves and a place to see.

Here I stand just inches tall,
It's twelve to be exact.
Looking around, more I see,
At times the height I lack.

Over the rise there, here too,
Some are yellow, red, blue, and green.
Tiny lanterns to guide their way,
Many more of them I have seen.

I took a walk into the woods,
For more I stumbled upon.
Colourful and short, they all appeared,
Many more were stepped on.

Too numerous to count or do the math,
An equation is what I seek.
Perhaps one day, my abilities I need,
Polynomials, a wonderous treat.

A CONNECTION WITH STRINGS ATTACHED

A child's perspective, years ago,
Walking to school in the cold.
The snow that fell, inches it'd rise,
Falling from the heavens and the sky.

For on this day, years ago,
Walking to school, everybody knows.
The snow that fell, chilled to the bone,
Walking in foot-deep snow alone.

Growing up with a band of kids,
Losing winter stuff, God forbid!
To make ends meet, keeping us alive,
Trying innovative ideas, my mom tried.

For on my face, Vaseline was lathered,
Too young to notice, it didn't matter.
Atop my head, a hat now chosen,
To lose it now, you will be frozen!

My mittens had a unique set rule,
Losing one was not cool.
Keeping hands warm was a real trick,
Losing one, watch out, the wooden stick.

Making ends meet, Mom learned to sew,
For knitting, a talent for, make money flow.
Mittens for a set, and five pairs to create,
The colour and style, up to debate.

A creative way to keep hands warm,
The string connected each mitten form.
From one sleeve attached to the coat,
To the other end, a means, a knitted rope.

Almost a mile, the walk began,
Climbing up the hill was the plan.
Waiting for a sign and snow to stop,
Wanting to break trail, or so I thought.

Up the hill, my little legs tired,
How steep is the hill, much higher.
With lunch in hand and a special treat,
Fluff-filled crackers, nothing can beat.

Finally, the end was almost in sight,
Seeing the trail was such a delight.
The building of bricks, all being red,
A place to undress, and nap instead.

THIS THING CALLED LOVE

Within the smile, perhaps a tear,
Within each day, the warmth is near.
Caring and patience, within just one,
The bonds that's carried is special to some.

Of mother and child and special friends,
The feeling is found and carried within.
Through the trials, though it all,
There comes a challenge within us all.

More than magic, a sense of pride,
When laughter is found deep inside.
Within the silence, a sense of peace,
Encourages to find the inner peace.

There are days when tempers flare,
When there are problems, it's hard to bear.
There are moments, they exist because,
When there are feuds, there is the love.

When in doubt, or perhaps confused,
Remember a hug, you cannot lose.
Perhaps one day, the time will come,
To find the magic, this thing called love.

CHRIS GODDARD "SILVERGHOST"

BBQED TO A STEAK DINNER

Peter, the farmer, was not his intent,
Working at St. Joe's was worth every cent.
Raising a family, two kids to raise,
Wife, Sandra, making sacrifices every day.

Victoria had a horse and a place to stay,
Bordering her up north was an easier way.
With a cottage nearby, weekends to stay,
A chance to go riding, a happier day.

Pete did retire to a place up north,
To this very farm, to care for the horse.
Acquiring a crop, to make ends meet,
The famer in him, an adventurous feat.

The farm that grew, many years to acquire,
To raise some animals, an income his desire.
Horses, cows, donkeys, and farmer Pete,
Historic barn built; he's not admitting defeat.

Pete and Christian raised a great feast,
Through wind and rain and farmer Pete.
He stood and stared, gazing into the barn,
A friend or foe meant him no harm.

Raised from a calf, work was desired,
Feedings every day, his name was inspired.
Months he grew, eight-hundred-pounds well deserved,
BBQ is his name, all covered in brown fur.

Just a week from now, BBQ will be retired,
Live out his years in a pasture desired.
Perhaps with the price of choice beef,
A butcher's hand may be his defeat.

Farmer Pete and a well-deserved feast,
Fired up the BBQ, medium-rare beast.
One last photo is all that remains,
BBQ the cow is now up in flames.

LES OR MORE, IT'S PRETTY COULES

In her spare time, this comes to mind,
A venue that all would meet.
Not long ago, where Les' talents show,
The BBQ smoke show a treat.

A place so, Coules, for here Dave rules,
Sensations and a place to chill.
The jazz sets a beat, a wonderous treat,
Dinner, drinks, and friends, better still.

Elements, a fifth of perfection, in perfect direction,
The Leader calls him Dave, he's Coules.
He sets the tone on tenor saxophone,
The tempo soothing and still rules.

An avenue, a treat, a respite retreat,
For Les is more even still.
The music so grand, the jazz quintet band,
A feeling it brings, a place to chill.

Les' part and the band leader heart,
She's one who coordinates the scenes.
Checking in friends, helping to no ends,
The moments sharing in their dreams.

If not for Dave, in his talented ways,
The leader, the conductor, so Coules.
Calibration within notes, arrangements he wrote,
Togetherness, their love still rules.

A moment to ponder, a while longer,
For memories of the music still rules.
Take this to heart, when Dave is a part,
Les or more, it's pretty Coules.

CHAPTER 16
CREATIVITY EXPLAINED

IPHONE, I SEE THE POSSIBILITIES

The iPhone I found, it's been around,
A thought that comes to mind.
Is it smart, beginning at the start?
An invention to save some time.
What can it do, the possibilities, it's new?
Connection, all these cumbersome tasks.
Numbers in a book, searching pages, you have looked!
The iPhone a quick search at last.
A snap of a friend, a memory to send,
A connection you have to the past.
The data to create, a moment to forsake,
A time on the phone once you grasp.
A connection to life, new tasks despite,
Relearning technology all over again.
A variety of apps, endless challenge perhaps,
Storage to consider before full ends.
The iPhone inspires, within each, a desire,
From 4 to 15, on to the end.
Create in ways, monthly fees to wage,
Its complexity and possibilities to lend.
Is it a must, your whole life you trust?
The information stored on the cloud.
To lose a friend, the iPhone will lend,
Memories to view this is allowed.
Millions of apps, endless perhaps,
To the store where they are found.
A price, a fee, is nothing ever free,
Icons now appear, emojis are 'round.
Passwords, a memory, will lapse,

The code, remembering it now.
Phone number in past, twenty-five you'd grasp,
One touch, it's even easier now.
Technologies we grasp, communication a task,
Android or iPhone is a choice.
Sending a text, yet brief and yet,
In the end, a preference to voice.
Inspiration to grasp knowledge will surpass,
Games too numerous to pursue.
Lost time on the device and quality of life,
Wordscapes, Wordle, many to review.

BLACKROCK: A FISHING TALE AS A KID

The sun shone bright, the day had begun,
Sitting all by myself, this memory just one.
Waiting, watching, and wanting to try,
Five kids to show, you get one try.
With the lucky rod in hand, a reel to partake,
Catching a fish, and the struggle it takes.
The line was fed through these little holes,
Away from the end to the reel it holds.
A hook, lead weight tied to the end of my line,
Waiting for the bait to sink took time.
A float was placed four feet from the end,
Red and white ball and a hook to suspend.
White Styrofoam bowl and opaque lid,
Within this contained, this bait lives.
The lid removed, the dirt seemed moist,
Long, thin, slippery worm, a bait of choice.
Huge in size, longer than my hand,
Long, thin worm emerged in hand.
Slithering, slippery, this, a last view,
Long, sharp hook, she ran it through.
Another jab, the blood inside gushed,
Farwell, Mr. Worm, I wished him luck.
Into the water, the worm was gone,
The ball of red and white floated along.
Minutes passed, nothing I could do,
Waiting, watching, with a humbled brood.
The ball soon sank, a tug on the line,
I yanked on the lucky rod, the fight was mine.
Reeling in with all my might,

Fight to the end, a fish was in sight,
Down it went, or so I thought,
The ball vanished beneath black rock.
I yanked again and reeled some more,
I reeled and reeled, this was a chore.
My arms now tired, I am not giving in,
This is my time, as darkness crept in.
A final tug, the fish soon appeared,
With a net in hand, dinner was near.
Brown and small, my rock bass caught,
Small, though too small, I thought.
The hook was removed, the fish let go,
One day soon, bigger he will grow.
If not for Mrs. Rallis, a friend of my folks,
The story of fishing, as thought provokes.
She showed us five kids just how to fish,
Walking on the rocks a memorable wish.
Place the worm upon each hook's line,
Looking back fifty-two years, a memory of mine.

SO THE JOURNEY BEGINS AGAIN RENEWED

*How to describe what is felt inside,
Remembering how to dream.
The emotions stirred, uttering few words,
Forgetting how it will seem.*

*Looking for a place, just any space,
A chance just to get away.
To look for a retreat, a faraway seat,
To relax hesitation portrays.*

*Time has passed, too long perhaps,
How long has this been?
Life dashed, precious moments slashed,
To go outside and dream.*

*To plan in place, a happier state,
Experience life just once more.
A sense to be, finally breaking free,
Two years, I've lost the score.*

*A cruise perhaps, too many souls, I'll pass,
To book an escape somewhere.
Book a flight, many people not right,
A place up north seems fair.*

*No mask in place, makeup will replace,
My soul renewed; inside I've reached.
A challenge to explore, the great outdoors,
Connecting, just beyond, I seek.*

Reconnect with friends, this moment lends,
Remembering how it will be.
A call is placed, in a calming state,
This moment to finally be free . . .

THE EARLY DAYS BACK IN SCHOOL

Let's go back in time, many years ago,
We're all so young, not long or so.
Remembering when innocence was bliss,
Envious of those days, now we miss.

Lunch was made, in a plain brown sack,
Peanut butter and jam, no turning back.
The lucky few, a lunch box, a case,
Thermos inside, with soup, no waste.

An invention for us, a means to control,
Marshmallow fluff, a rush for the soul.
Between two crackers, a layer of treasure,
Biting into them, an exquisite pleasure.

Catholic system, with rules to abide,
Dressing for success, along for the ride.
Those of us were blessed with style,
A uniform chosen and seen for miles.

The hour of eight, Monday had arrived,
Get up, eat breakfast, rules to abide.
The lucky few, walking was no gift,
The rest of us, didn't get a lift.

We stand at attention, a daily roll,
Here, present, he's sick, takes its toll.
Singing national anthem, or trying to,
A cumbersome task, a daily review.

Learning to read, the ability to spell,
Remembering the letters, challenging as well.
Cursive writing, cumbersome for some,
Gripping a pencil challenged everyone.

The lucky few, learning to write,
Right hand chosen, no ruling despite.
Being left-handed was a curse,
Smack on the wrist, could do no worse.

With ink and quill, the rights had form,
Lefthanded, a wicked force conforms.
Witchcraft, the writing, was believed,
To change the ways, to save, indeed.

Misbehaving, was a cardinal rule,
Off to the office, in my school.
On the wall, the principal's strap,
Bend over and pray, fear will lapse.

The spelling bee, as all did try,
Hoping to be skipped, who would decide.
Standing by the board, chalk in hand,
All eyes staring, one lonesome fan.

When tired, a rest was required,
Lying on the floor, a nap desired.
Really for teachers, a quiet place,
Chance to refresh, in a peaceful state.

Hour of nine, the school in session,
Reading, writing, math, history in question.
A break for recess, lunch for rest,
At four the bell rang, a day to test.

Tag, hopscotch, a game of catch,
Running, exhaustion, endurance at best.
Just like gym class, a challenge to some,
Climbing up the rope, my fear, this one!

Walking to school, uphill both ways,
A mere two feet high and no snow days.
In winter, a challenge, clothing restricts,
Layers of warmth, this was the pits.

For those of us, many years now lapsed,
A moment in time, too many have passed.
Fond memories, as the photos reflect,
Black and white, colour, in retrospect.

THE RED FRUIT FROM A TO Z

Adoration, the fruit of choice,
A cocktail selection, tasters voiced.
Brandywine, mortgage lifter, I'm in,
The fruit of summer, warmth sets in.

Campari, a mountain magic seeds,
They are priceless at 150K, all agreed.
Early girl, she is dependable and prolific,
Cultivated for cold and dry, so delicious.

Fourth of July, this boastful fruit,
Planted early, a celebration to boot.
Great white and gardeners delight,
Creamy globes, up two pounds, out of sight.

Hanover, not the size where it's grown,
The seed are plain, near to home.
Japanese black trifle, burgundy in hue,
An edible snack in a salad too.

Lillian's yellow heirloom, the pallet bright,
The flavour exquisite and meaty bite.
Money-maker, cash crop, a farmer's delight,
Scores of the red fruit, the choice is right.

Pantano Romanesco, an Italian flavour,
Grown with love, a table-intense favour.
Rebellion, textured lines, salads will rejoice,
Mediterranean, when stuffed by choice.

Santorini, first harvested in Greece,
One-of-a-kind, delicious, and sweet.
Tomaccio, a wild Peruvian, a true feast,
Best dried and stored, intense and sweet.

Yellow pear, of yellow, orange, and red,
Colourful and bright, or so it's been said.
Zebra colour is seen of yellow and green,
Grown to perfection, this fruit is green.

All who still wonder what this poem is about,
Ask Ms. Dugo, her expertise, no doubt.
This time, every year, to the nursery she drives,
Planting this red fruit, a feast for the eyes.

PAINT BY NUMBERS; TO THE PAINTER'S PLACE

Within the box, a surprise awaits,
Until it opens, with undue haste.
Wrapping and package, sealed tight,
From wandering eyes, day and night.

The open box reveals a canvas in white,
With lines and numbers, a feeling delight.
The tray of paint, twelve colours in all,
A brush to paint, awaits one and all.

Following the instructions, a creative task,
Awaits the artist, as the hours pass.
Number by number, the paint is applied,
Choosing each colour, the vision resides.

With brush in hand, each stroke reveals,
The artist's work, within concealed.
Hours it seems, the creation awaits,
For artists alike, the patience debates.

Within each stoke, creativity sparked,
Detailed lines, feelings from the heart.
With the last brush, the paint will dry,
The canvas complete, displayed with pride.

With easel set, the canvas in white,
The image within the artist ignites.
Colours create the images displayed,
A landscape, pond, a vacation stay.

Knowledge challenged, a dream revealed,
A creative approach, the love appeals.
Corresponding numbers of colours alike,
Remembering each one, a creative insight.

Collection created, with inspiration drawn,
Creative selections, numerically, will spawn.
Off-white colours correspond to a dream,
Applied to the walls, a loving home's scene.

Moore Classics chosen, a colour conforms,
When applied to the surface, feeling warms.
Historical colours, a creation to wage,
A sensation now seen, an historical age.

An Affinity collection, within warm tones,
A cool selection, close to home.
Designer Classics, with a creative flare,
Inspiration created, with Tom to share.

The creator of colour, pizzazz, and insight,
To meet the man, an inquisitive right.
With years of experience, an eye for detail,
He will inspire the vision in every detail.

The images and tones, the warmth drawn,
The love of colours, a sense to belong.
Humbled to the core, a wonder desired,
Mr. Tom Marino, a creative ability inspired.

WHIRLIGIG, WHATCHAMACALLIT; YOU KNOW WHAT I MEAN?

How to describe that thing, I decide,
It's on the tip of my tongue.
I stick it out, still blurry, I shout!
I cannot see it or anyone.

Whatchamacallit word you will have heard,
You know what I mean.
I have written it down, it cannot be found,
Looking everywhere, still not seen.

Tongue-tied and distraught, now it's lost,
Where can I look to find?
I just put it down, can it be found?
Lost for hours, time to unwind.

That thing on my mind, it's all the time,
I walked into the room, now what?
A loss of thought, my mind is shot,
Returning the hammer, I have brought.

I check my phone, I am not alone,
The number, the code, to recall.
I cannot lie, hard as I try,
Blasted number, I'm done with it all.

Am I that far gone; I don't belong?
That blasted thing is the death of me.
Looking in every drawer, flabbergasted, what for?
Without my spectacles, I cannot see.

Lying down for a rest, I've done my best,
Looking in every crevice known to man.
I wake in the night, turning on the light,
Looking around, awestruck, suddenly, damn!

Rushing to my feet, lighter, I leaped,
Remembering to where the Whirligig's placed.
Whatchamacallit was seen, gobsmacked, it's green,
The tea infuser holder is out of place.

A NOVEL IDEA IN THE SIXTIES TO THE PRESENT

<u>Take away was a math problem</u>
For most of us, a term often used,
Back in the day, this term was new.
Subtraction in math, a means to reduce,
Taking away had nothing to lose.

A means to transport food from a store,
Packages now used are cheap to afford.
From pizza to salads, sushi to soup,
These containers are preferred and abused.

<u>Pizza was something to do with a leaning tower</u>
The leaning tower of Pisa, the tower stands,
The way in which it's viewed, confusion demands.
For hundreds of years the tower was viewed,
Thousands still visited, a marvel it drew.

The tower of pizza, the dough never used,
The slope to the tower, all were confused.
No oven to cook, no toppings were made,
Still it's sloped, the young remain dazed.

<u>Rice eaten as pudding</u>
A dessert, a treat, made with rice,
A creative way to promote and entice.
Rice, milk, eggs, sugar, and cream,
Bring to a boil, let cool, what a dream.

White or brown, something in between,
A sidekick for meat, fish is what it seems.
The white texture just boils up,
A pot of water, a side dish ... right?

<u>Curry was a surname not a spice</u>
What's in a name? Curry just the same,
A surname is all that was used.
A name purposed only for those,
Unique, special, understood, I suppose.

A robust flavour, created and savoured,
A spice added to sweeten the pot.
An Indian spice, created and delighted,
Its fragrance confused, most will not.

<u>Calamari was a fish used as bait</u>
White, long, and found in the sea,
Used as bait, as fishermen will agree.
Italian for squid, calamari is derived,
Catch coalfish, dogfish, and bass soon realized.

It's long and skinny, the slippery type,
Tasty when cooked, fried just right.
Appetizer or main course, a feast for the eyes,
Don't knock it until you have tried.

<u>The TV was b & w, with no remote</u>
Big box in the corner, with legs attached,
Getting up to change it, with dial attached.
To change the channel, a daunting task,
Black and white, rabbit ears in the back.

Screen so thin, it hangs on the wall,
Thousands of channels, remembering them all.
Wireless, remote, with batteries within,
Losing the remote, you're now done in.

<u>Cooking outside was called camping</u>
Going up north, an adventure to drive,
The great outdoors and cooking outside.
Pitching a tent, a Coleman stove set,
Cooking in the outdoors, camping the best.

Set a fire in the oven to bake,
Pizza is made, mosquitoes forsake.
Back of the house, open the door,
Convenience of home, what's camping for?

<u>We never had elbows or phones at the table</u>
The table is set, all gather here,
The family together, we pray here.
Dinner at six is set in stone,
No elbows at the table, sets the tone.

Whether it's five, six, or seven, no one's home,
No one eats together, we all eat alone.
Elbows on the table, etiquette is gone,
Phones at the table, silence now belongs.

<u>A cassette tape and a pencil to rewind</u>
The way of music, a cassette was created,
To store our music, this was debated.
Device to record, catching the tape again,
Pencil to the rescue, spooling, rewinding in vain.

iTunes, mp3, digital recording alike,
Small, efficient, oh, such a delight.
Thousands of songs, efficient too,
Too young to remember, an insignificant brute.

A glimpse of the ages, changes in store,
Remembering our past in photographs and more.
Technology through the years, how each view,
Explaining how it worked, this poem proved.

UNIQUE, UP BEFORE YOU'RE DISCOVERED.

Paths, worn-down ruts on the route,
This farmer cares, his endless pursuit.
The dawn comes, the chores to be done,
Getting up early, just before the sun.

As the sun sets, the farmer has retired,
Success of his labour, an organic desire.
Ready for harvest, the market awaits,
Last night to prepare for picking waits.

I sneak up slowly, a step at a time,
Looking both ways, waiting for a sign.
The gate ajar, the basket awaits,
Timing is right, the bounty to taste.

The sun was setting, the sky red,
All darlings snuggled asleep in their bed.
The gate opened and vegetables on display,
No one to guard, I can have my way.

A tall wooden pole rises to the sky,
Cheerful scarecrow, dressed to surprise.
Over the rise, the cornstalks in a row,
The ears are plentiful, my selection grows

Remembering the rule, walk in ten rows,
Avoid the feed corn, icky taste to know.
On the top of the stalk, the silk turns brown,
Corn perfect for picking, quietly, shh!, no sound.

Tomatoes are ripe, yellow, orange, and red,
Cucumbers are plump, beans overhead.
Spotting the red peppers and tears to the eyes,
Taking a bite, true flavour is realized.

Carrots for picking, kale a real treat,
Spinach for salads, chives is what I seek.
Hours of care, a creation for soup,
Many choices and endless pursuit.

A sweet smell, the nostrils awoke,
Small berries to savour and provoke.
Blueberries, blackberries, strawberries alike,
Cranberries, mulberries, mouth-watering delight.

Baskets now full, the harvest awaits,
Walking across the field, the farmer waits.
Caught in the act, my plan now dashed,
Pay for the goods or put them back.

LIFE WITHIN A DREAM; THE STORY CONTINUES

With awe and wonder, a sense of desire,
The love of one and inspiration inspired.
Each aspect of life as one is drawn,
Waiting and watching, feelings spawn.

A look of surprise, the feeling is shown,
Within a deep feeling, the love has grown.
Within each day, another will dawn,
A sensation is growing, and it belongs.

Within the spark, within the desire,
Imagination is influenced even higher.
Across the room and image sparked,
Over time the feelings as one embarked.

A simple hello and called by name,
Nervousness drawn out soon changed.
A simple pleasure within two words,
Response to the feeling warmth deserves.

As dating progresses the feelings grow,
The sensation inside the light glows.
With each passing day another to come,
Until the day a couple you become.

A call is placed to ask for her hand,
Willing parents now have a plan.
One day to return an island affair,
Sao Miguel Island, they'll be married there.

Within the magic each day is shared,
Family and friends are made aware.
A special night the one to propose,
With a ring secured, nervousness flows.

The night is set in a creative affair,
A hidden photographer made aware.
Location selected, the rooftop scene,
Red carpet displays the scene.

A walk to the edge, flashes appear,
Down on one knee, so does the tears.
A few simple words, the emotion stirred,
A poignant moment, a pause is heard.

Upon the finger the ring is placed,
A hug and emotions cannot be replaced.
A kiss to seal the endless embrace,
The photographer views photos in haste.

BREAKFAST OF CHAMPIONS; RETIRED, FINALLY

To hell with the bell, that sounds neat,
Welcoming for breakfast, a wonderous treat.
Attendance not taken, no teaching required,
No helping after school, now happily retired.

No prep or marking, no exams to write,
No early mornings, no traffic to fight.
No café duty or covering a class,
Waiting for the copier, making copies last.

A place we visit, not far from here,
Meeting monthly, a place and good cheer.
The hour of ten, a challenge for some,
Finding a table for twenty-four is cumbersome.

Thanks to Sharon, coordinating us all,
Weeks in advance, remembering to call.
A challenge for some, the list has grown,
Email everyone, for technology unknown.

Many years they've gathered, more to come,
Memories savoured, remembering each one.
Chosen few celebrate breakfast this way,
The first Monday of the month, this very day.

This place to eat, catch up with friends,
An hour or so, our time we'll spend.
Faces, places, vacations still await,
Photos of grandkids or moments to partake.

Newly retired and welcome to partake,
The newest one's young memories to make.
COVID has dashed our time and fears,
Two years and waiting, at last we're here.

The tradition continues, each month to rejoice,
A simple gesture, an ability to voice.
A smiling face to remember and recall,
Let's give thanks, a toast to one and all.

Those who are new, this place we gather,
The Daylight Grill just retired, no matter.
This location is chosen, for now you seek,
Royal Windsor and Southdown a seniors' retreat.

THE THREE OF US, EXPLAINED

Not often said, some who dread,
A lack of understanding, until now.
Trying to succeed, surviving the need,
Needing more hands, somehow.

When you require a hand, alone you stand,
Needing help with a task at hand.
Ability to succeed, outweighs the need,
Reality within your ability demands.

Thoughts come to mind, perhaps just mine,
The meaning of what I will explain.
More often than not, for me just a thought,
The meaning of us, just three, is insane.

Standing in the room, for three, you'd assume,
The answer correct is not.
Three are aware, have and to care,
It is nine, the equation has brought.

How do you surmise, go figure, realize,
How does three become nine?
I will explain, you many refrain,
It's easy and simple yet in time.

The three of us know, we are allowed,
The answer to the question concludes.
It's me, myself, and I, as we still try,
The final answer is real news.

THE MILKMAN AND THE DOOR IN THE WALL

The morning had come, the sun rose,
Today, our delivery excitement arose.
The man in white, with baskets galore,
Within its contents, a grocery store.

In the distance, the bells would ring,
Even closer the truck theme he'd bring.
Dressed in white and a cap in sight,
Walking up the driveway, what a delight.

The large basket measured two by two,
Milk, cream, butter for a happy brood.
In the wall, a small door was here,
Square in shape, the contents appeared.

Surrounded by bricks, the box concealed,
Once opened, the contents were revealed.
Within the box, its contents stored,
Protected from elements, retrieved once more.

The glass of milk and cream on top,
The cap secured, but do not drop.
The cream was a treat, and thick it'd stay,
Added to coffee, the calories to weigh.

Within the wall, this box appeared,
We often wonder just why it was here.
Perhaps a way to sneak outside,
Small enough to squeeze inside.

The latch was placed to secure the way,
For curious kids might escape one day.
The bell was rung to remind us of all,
The milkman is here, a delivery call.

The hour of nine, this day had arrived,
This long-awaited visit, the milk had gone dry.
Seven mouths to feed, the milk was gone.
The milkman, a savior, four-gallons strong.

The door now opens, the glass in white,
Four bottles now stored, such a delight.
Milk, cream, butter, and lard,
History remembered, back then it was hard.

Into the cupboard, empty jugs stayed,
Until he returned, long-awaited day.
The truck was gone, another to arrive,
The breadman appeared, with the sweet surprise.

CACHE LAKE ANNUAL LEASEHOLDERS' REGATTA; THE CRAB RACE

The eighty-seventh annual regatta was held on the lake,
With fifty activities, the long weekend awaits.
The sun arose and the sky so blue,
Hundreds of participants, the excitement grew.

A visitor to Algonquin Park, for little I knew,
When asked to volunteer, my enthusiasm grew.
Scanning the horizon, anticipating the route,
Checking the competition, one chance I knew.

Bruce, a leaseholder, was in a bind,
He needed a volunteer; I arrive on time.
The strategy discussed and knowledge to lead,
My ability to participate, willingly I agreed.

A choice was made, a challenge for some,
The crab race we'd entered, ability to overcome.
The canoe was placed in the water's edge,
A moment to ponder, as rules we read.

Chris in the bow and Bruce at the stern,
Paddling with only hands, a technique learned.
Kneeling position set, to focus on the end,
Defending for the right, waiting 'round the bend.

A moment of silence, the excitement grew,
What have I done, my nervousness I knew?
Looking down at the water, an uneasiness begins,
Not seeing the bottom, hesitation creeps in.

Minutes passed as I spoke out loud,
Swimming in clear waters, what happens now?
The course was ready, my thoughts cleared,
Ready for the crab race, the seconds neared.

On your mark, get set, and go!
Crab race was on, the winner, who knows.
Head down, focused on the race,
Paddling faster, inching closer in haste.

We had the lead, others closing in,
My heart racing, excitement within.
Turners edging closer, as we held our own,
The gap now widening, racing for home.

Farther behind, the Turners seemed to be,
Each stroke a victory, in a moment we'd see.
The lead so vast, no competitor was near,
To the victor, the red ribbon first appeared.

Finish line approached, closer each stroke,
I'm not giving up, as my thoughts invoked.
Dripping wet and soaked to the skin,
The end nearer, a monumental win.

The crab race was a challenge for some,
Volunteers and participants, everybody won.
Ribbons were given, another year was done,
Trophies to the victors, next year they'd come.

CACHE LAKE: A GREAT ESCAPE

Excitement awaits on the island estate,
A few more hours to drive.
Through the gates, the parking lot waits,
The effort is worth it if you decide.

A parking pass or seasonal pass,
Either way, parking here is not free.
A challenge for some to overcome,
The next step, a challenge, you'll see.

The parking lot and finding a spot,
Now that you've finally arrived.
Off-loading your ride, effort, you've tried,
Walking to the edge to decide.

To search for a ride, which one you decide,
Along the shore, the canoes lie.
With paddle in hand, you leave this land,
Paddling to the island with pride.

With wind and rain, you never complain,
The sun, the snow, and cold.
Life on the lake, the challenges it takes,
Living on the lake is never old.

Paddling a skill, technique, and will,
Remembering the first time you tried.
Closer you get, you never forget,
Soon arrived on the island with pride.

Life on the lake, it gives and takes,
Challenges in our lives each day.
The basic needs, as some disagree,
The cottage, memories we wage.

Within a day or two, taking in the view,
Remembering, for the memories return.
The years have passed, you're home at last,
Life lessons we live and learn.

The great escape, Cache Lake awaits,
Making memories, one at a time.
Island life, its challenge ignites,
A step back, it's simple, every time.

THE BEAT OF THE DRUM FALLS SILENT, RELIGIOUSLY

This day had come, especially for one,
For Mark, his time has come.
A teacher for years, religiously drumming here,
Today we celebrate one so young.

Leader of the band, he's in good hands,
The drums have silenced as well.
Drumsticks raised, the heavens are praised,
A teacher and philosopher for a spell.

The final day, kneel and pray,
The drummer's last gig is complete.
Exams marked, report card embarked,
The door is closed, time to sleep.

Lounge singers began, serenading the man,
The gambler, his day has begun.
A spiritual sign, time to resign,
Cashed in his chips, he's now done.

Through guidance he arrived, religiously he survived,
Though sound following the light.
Students were taught, life skills brought,
Time and praise are here tonight.

One by one, all did succumb,
Religion, philosophy, God-given right.
Praise of a man, all would understand,
Mark's shown his guiding light.

Each story began, soul searching in hand,
Within each a personal story shared.
The crew their right, Mark's teaching did ignite,
Emotional stories made aware.

Years he has taught, life lessons brought,
Bronson's band the sounds a treat.
Drumsticks are a tool, rhythm a rule,
The heart of a man with a beat.

A moment to ponder, for Mark a while longer,
Retirement, the next chapter, now begins.
He leaves his mark, in each of our hearts,
Philosopher religiously from here on in.

THE OUTHOUSE, IN THE GREAT OUTDOORS

The place outside, the place to hide,
This place a means to go.
Shed with a roof, a place to poop,
Sweet aroma seems to flow.

Hidden it seems, a place of dreams,
Screened in to avoid the bite.
Mosquitoes will fly, scheming they try,
Motionless, your focus their plight.

The window to view, the forest to poo,
Patience in silence it seems.
When nature calls, beware above all,
The outhouse is not what it's been.

Setting your sights, the middle of the night,
Cozy and snuggled in bed.
The urge to pee some disagrees,
The challenge disregard instead.

The moons in bed, exhausted you dread,
The howl heard in the night.
Do you embark, afraid of the dark?
The fear unknown tonight.

The pressure within, the kidneys begin,
The power to let it flow.
Each step taken, now forsaken,
Finally, a change to let go.

Remembering a thought, the headlamp you brought,
A light and the ability to see.
Batteries now dead, the moment you dread,
The need, your hands now free.

Finding the door, quite a chore,
Darkness the building surrounds.
The handle secured, just one word,
Inside no toilet paper found.

A scream in the night, terror to fight,
Toilet paper, the roll is cruel.
Awakened and dazed, making your way,
Next time indoor toilet a rule.

Silence abounds, suddenly a sound,
Motionless, fear sets in.
How long do you wait, minutes to debate?
The odour, the fragrance, begins.

Follow the trail, the effluent beware,
The heat and humidity begin.
The ability to flush, there is no rush,
Into the deep where nature begins.

Whether it rains, you cannot complain,
The bathroom is not inside.
The great outdoors, at times a chore,
Challenged there's no place to hide.

This place you roam, far from home,
When nature calls, you go.
Memories it seems, lost in our dreams,
Just going with the flow.

THROUGH THE LENS TO THE CANVAS

Through the lens she takes, the images to create;
Ideas as nature brings into sight.
Paintings to express, with pastel no less;
The photograph now brought to life.

Hours she drives, to the location that thrives;
To view all that nature displays.
With tools at hand, surveying the land;
For the easel a place to stay.

Blank canvas in white, an image to ignite;
The challenge, hours to invest.
Patience and time, the image resigns;
Time on the road, nonetheless.

With a map in hand, venturing to new lands;
Creativity and insight brought to life.
Inspiration, knowledge spared; the painting shared;
Intuitiveness of the artist's insight.

A walk on the shore, the landscape to explore;
What nature has created today.
The flow of the land over hills to expand;
Inspiration and a painting one day.

Trees and flowers, she searches for hours;
Whether summer, winter, spring, or fall.
Streams flow, over the rocks into coves;
Creative insight for one and all.

Inspired each day, works of art to display;
On the walls, galleries, and homes.
Commissions acquired, the love and desire;
Catherine brings new appreciation home.

Her passion a desire, in students she inspires;
Creating classes for artists is one part.
Hours she spends, creating lessons to lend;
Years teaching photography and art.

THANK COD FOR NEWFOUNDLAND

From coast to coast, the sea life boasts,
The cod, the fishing is second to none.
In 1492 fish was caught, no one thought,
One day overfishing would be done.
Five hundred years, the cod stock disappeared,
Fishing near Newfoundland was one.
A way of life, overfishing despite,
The end of cod fishing for everyone.
This way of life had changed in spite,
Fishing on the island, the cod stock ceased.
Fisherman would resound, fishing did rebound,
Soon crab and shrimp had increased.
Twenty years passed, the cod fishing relapsed,
With a limit on how much was to be caught.
The cycle of life, cod fishing did ignite,
Newfoundlanders, they never forgot.
For miles around, fishing villages are found,
Homes on the cliffs by the sea.
Lobster season is done, cod season's begun,
Newfoundland hospitality now believed.
The fish of choice, few others will voice,
For cod fresh from the sea.
Into the deep, a mere twelve hundred feet,
A tasty meal by any feast.
Fish and chips, only cod, this fish,
Jigging, trolling, or going deep.
July through September, thirty-nine days to remember,
The challenge a weekend fisherman's treat.
Three days of the week, cod fishing they seek,

Five fish each a day for the prize.
Cleaned and smoked, an iceberg beer toast,
Frozen for the winters with pride.
A tradition for most, a humbling toast,
Honorary Newfoundland is required.
Kiss the cod, a shot, of screech was thought,
Dead fish, Jamaican barrel drink desired.
Those who reside, the island with pride,
From land, sea, and fishing boats.
A way of life, feeding families alike,
Thank Cod for Newfoundland folks.

THE ROCK BY THE SEA, NEWFOUNDLAND

There is a place, though far from here,
Over land there is no route.
Travelling by air, for ferry if you dare,
An island with a rugged pursuit.

The mountain stands and the table lands,
Seeing the mantle of the earth.
This land remains, a hiker's terrain,
Rocky grounds so dry it still thirsts.

On the edge of the coast, a lighthouse boasts,
The warming light is still seen.
Shipping is a means, the island of dreams,
Surrounded by the sea it's been.

Water surrounds, the rocky island abounds,
The towering cliff of stone.
Thrashed by waves, reshaping each day,
Desolate yet never alone.

Where icebergs roam, far from home,
Whales in search of food.
Twenty-two species are found, searching around,
Raising the young healthy brood.

Newfoundland pride, a rhythmic side,
For those who cannot play a note.
Ugly stick was created, designed, and debated,
Its creativity in drinking it boasts.

Branch from the tree, five foot decreed,
Soup can head painted, mop on top.
Beer caps in a row, the nails to hold,
Spaced three inches apart, cropped.

With a boot on the foot, a challenge mistook,
The ugly stick was now created.
A handle is notched, with beer caps atop,
This instrument is still debated.

Wildlife roams, not far from home,
Moose in thousands are around.
In marshes and streams, many can be seen,
Vegetation consumed less is found.

This place to wander, a while longer,
St. Johns homes on Wellington Row.
Great fire erased, the structures saved face,
Rebuilding the homes as we know.

The colours displayed, a rainbow way,
Brightening the neighbourhood streets.
Bright colours favoured, ice cream shop flavours,
Just walking is a festive treat.

Island like no other, the hospitality to discover,
Newfoundland a destination for most.
Hunting is one source, fishing of course,
On this island food is caught, shot, or choked.

GETTING SCREECHED IN IS A THING, JUST ONCE

Give praise a thought, traditions brought,
An idea so messed up It is true.
A traditional toast, to the humble host,
Kiss a dead codfish sets the mood.

This idea began, on some far-off land,
Honorary Newfoundlander you will become.
Praise for the fish, endless bounty persists,
A feast celebrated by everyone.

Those who preach, two shots of screech,
Doing a jig, and ugly sticks required.
Kiss the codfish, if you wish,
Bon voyage on your journey desire.

As legends told, the story unfolds,
Serviceman goes in the bar for rum.
He howled so loud, looks from the crowd,
The strong bite surprised everyone.

The officer exclaimed, the noise refrained,
Newfoundland shouted Tis screech.
The Jamaican rum, forty percent my son,
In Scottish dialect screigh is screech.

Thousands of people flock, the island of rock,
Newfoundland a place by the sea,
A plaque on the wall, celebrated by all,
This place with so many memories.

LEFTHANDED, LEFTOVERS & LEFT BEHIND

Lefthanded is learned, ongoing concern,
Reasons though not yet proved.
Curvature of the hand, technique demands,
Creativity the decision renewed.

The ability to write, a challenge despite,
Having the ability to pursue.
The hand of choice, one right voice,
Left or right is still under review.

To aid or ease, the ability to please,
Ink and quill the words smear.
Create and instruct, rules as such,
It's wronged the words one hears.

The challenge for some, to overcome,
Meals another day to be used.
Leftovers less fuss, for the rest of us,
Choices for today less amused.

To search for a way, a mean to wage,
Stretching out food to last.
Meals today, extending in ways,
The price increases the gap.

Sunday night, reasons a delight,
An extra meal now saved.
Struggling each day, the time away,
Leftovers a love to wage.

The day has come, adventure for some,
A new destination awaits.
Log road ahead, exhausted you dread,
Left behind alone you debate.

Rise with the sun, getting work done,
Tasks too many to recall.
Each day stressed, remembering the rest,
Forgetting a task above all.

One place to discover, a place like no other,
How many kids are on the list.
Counting each head, tired you dread,
Left behind one kid you missed.

LOOKING FOR SUNLIGHT ON A DREARY DAY

Cache lake we seek, a break, a retreat,
That place up north remains.
Once we arrive, tension subsides,
Another season on the lake sustains.

The rains that came, the sun remained,
The clouds hung heavy and low.
Sky was dark, winds played there part,
Rivers once ebbed now flowed.

Ground now soaked, tempers invoked,
Getting to the island a treat.
With safety in mind, paddling over time,
A break in clouds, the rain ceased.

A challenge for some, the rain still comes,
The wood porch gets wet.,
As years it rains, swollen wood remains,
Slipping and sliding we forget.

Grab hold in the rain, to avoid the pain,
Hitting the porch on your butt.
As nature decides, forsaking your pride,
Rainy days at the cottage still sucks.

Trees all around, the canopy surrounds,
Hemlocks branch out to sustain.
The sun shines down, little light is found,
Coolness and shadows remain.

Views all around, stillness abounds,
Nothing like being on the lake.
Spring arrives as summer thrives,
Memories each year we make.

Autumn in near, cold winds appear,
Time on the lake must change.
Tamarack trees turn, needles spurn,
One hundred years family remains.

BITTEN BY THE CACHE LAKE BEE

Cache lake we arrived, rain now thrived,
The day now shortened our stay.
Clouds hung low, going with the flow,
Tomorrow is another day.

Hidden from view, months it grew,
Suspended ten feet from the ground.
Just walking by a yellow jacket flew by,
This unsuspecting home was found.

Bunkie was seen, painted newly green,
The eves now covered as well.
Below our sight, this ball did ignite,
Buzzing full of life for a spell.

Greyish hue, now seemingly glued,
Hidden away up out of sight.
Precariously it stayed, growing each day,
This nest was Bruce's plight.

Humming it seemed, louder it has been,
Activity the bees have thrived.
One gracious sole, his heart took hold,
To remove this deadly hive.

A plan in place, no time to debate,
The nest too large to avoid.
Approached he tried, moment of surprise,
A decision or skillful ploy.

With tools in hand, creativity demands,
Technics a keen sense of skill.
A board he attacked, bees fought back,
One sting then pain instilled.

The target the strike, the bee's last flight,
The stinger and the final blow.
The bee succumbed, death for one,
For age my agility now slowed.

A final dash, the pain now attacked,
The throbbing and swelling began.
With cortisone cream, Advil a dream,
The icing to freeze the pain.

My cheek turned blue, the swelling grew,
Searing pain, a dull ache resumed.
Lesson now learned, ongoing concern,
Next time safety concerns consume.

A thought to ponder, a while longer,
A mask may had lessened the pain.
An unavoidable sting, one less thing,
Next time I may refrain.

GREEN EFFECTS...

How to describe, this colour resides,
Buildings in all shapes and sizes.
Forests inspires, this paint desired,
Blending in with nature one tries.

A choice to choose, win or lose,
To colour, tint, and effect.
Samples to display, colours to wage,
Choices which we all respect.

In search of a store, with colours galore,
Selection of paints are in stock.
Collection of supplies, cost now realized,
Do you purchase or decide to walk.

Within the shed, lost colours bled,
With stains many cans still lie.
Oils once pursued, and no longer used,
Into the scrap pile they die.

Labels once read, now faded instead,
Prying opens the can, to gaze,
A simple stir, muttering those words,
Once liquid, a lump now displayed.

Years of sun, rain, warn out they remain,
Once vibrate facades now fades.
A splash of colour, renewed like no other,
Brought to life one day.

Hours it seems, the vision in a dream,
The time has finally come.
New England green, is not what it seems,
Its green is green for everyone.

Four gallons, stir sticks, does the trick,
Two coats of paint will decide
With a chance to cure, many days to observe,
One building down a sense of pride.

A VISIONARY AND SPIRITUAL ADVISOR

A visionary, entrepreneur searching here,
This place on Long Lake ideas did ignite.
Building a family business in Bala was clear,
A place called home sixties year of his life.

Looking across the horizon the lake so still,
Sun shines bright on this autumn day.
Three days each year a change to chill,
Happiness with friends sharing this way.

Our spiritual advisor a heavenly soul,
Practical jokes a sense of humour too.
Guiding our lives as each day unfolds,
The warming feeling, you feel it too.

Moments many of us now share,
Soft-spoken voice our memories she is around.
Now, we grin and bear,
As we gather our deep friendships found.

Those of us that gather here today,
Remembering those who have left a mark.
For Herb & Joanie have come this way,
Let us celebrate their lives in our hearts.

Remembering our friends, passed this way,
Their journey has now begun.
The next set step to discover today,
Remembering family, friends, everyone.

With smiles in our heart's tears in our eyes,
The stories, memories many to recall.
The candle jokes a smile realized,
A visionary, a nun above us all.

Spiritus guidance we look everyday,
Sharing laughter in our hearts.
We gather here to share a meal,
Thankful that we were a part.

THE STINGER IS REALLY A HARPOON

I waited and watched this tiny bee,
Flying around close by me.
Then he was gone in a flash,
Before I knew it, he was back.
Buzzing and floating in the air,
I wondered how he hovered there.
I moved in close getting a better view,
He had a friend, not one or two.
I followed him, to his home,
Far from here, now I am alone.
Over the lawn, up over the rise,
Down the laneway was I surprised!
Not one or two, three or five,
He has friends, outnumbered was I.
I realized I invaded their hood,
I ran away as fast as I could.
My tiny little legs, were all that I had,
These tiny little bees were mad.
My heart pounding, my legs gave out,
I was done for it, all tuckered out.
Then a harpoon, pierced my butt,
Long steel dagger began to erupt.
Searing jolt, I shouted in pain,
Trying to run my legs aflame.
I ran to mommy, dropped my pants,
Looking at the dagger, a quick glance.
Harpoon was long throbbing too,
Doused with alcohol dads home brew.
Into the sewing basked, a needle was chosen,

Disinfected my butt sensation now frozen.
Don't move, hold still, this won't hurt.
One poke, two, soon you get dessert.
Within the tweezers, this harpoon was free,
The blood now oozing down to my knee,
Thin and tiny the dagger tossed aside,
Bee's stinger tyranny I have survived.

IT HAPPENED ONE NIGHT

The sun was bright, relief was in sight,
The clouds hung heavy and low.
The winds blew, as a cold witch's brew,
The night now dark for bode.

Rain that came, snow now reigned,
The icicles hung heavy and low.
Windows shook, as an old fisherman's crook,
Night now darkened turned cold.

Fire that warmed, dowsed by the storm,
Shivering and soaked to the bone.
No paper to light, no warmth to ignite,
Now doomed, desolate and alone.

Door slammed shut, door handle stuck,
The grip of cold remained.
A tree branch crashed, the window smashed,
One night uneasiness changed.

The sky once black, never changed back,
Eerily in the sky a green hue.
Roar of the train, in the distance sustained,
Still closer the intense storm grew.

Sleet and snow, covered the road,
The thundering echoes remained.
No sign of life, no candlelight,
This night would not be the same.

A single breath, a challenge no less,
The warmth rose to the sky.
The walls cracked, like broken down shack,
This night farewell and goodbye.

The flash of white, a brilliant sight,
The house began to shake.
The flash of light, the sky did ignite,
Tonight, to have and forsake.

A spark of light, a dimly lit fight,
Crystals of ice filled every gap.
Fire consumed, this grip of gloom,
The cold was fading back.

Over the rise, the thunderous skies,
Flashes too numerous were seen.
The rained ceased, with wind decreased,
On this night a scary scene.

The sun arose, the roads still closed,
The roof above was gone,
These souls survived, all still alive,
Today we fight and move on.

GYM

There is a place, not far from this space,
Where lights and sounds outweigh.
With machines to improve, the way we move,
Strengthening and slimming our way.

The price we pay, to shape in ways,
To improve our overall health.
The days to train, next day to complain,
In the end our physique is stealth.

Clothing a choice, reflects our voice,
The expense is draining our wealth.
Getting in shape, a choice to make,
To extend our long-term health.

The pool a space, cooling embrace,
Exercising and a means to cool.
Lengths we take, each stoke we make,
The distance over time still rules.

With classes to improve, music to groove,
Yoga stretching out our limits.
Spinning your way, cycling each day,
Getting out what you put in it.

Free weights to gain, muscles will remain,
Pumping iron setting the bar.
The time of the day, health to weigh,
In the end your ahead by far.

THE VIEW THROUGH THE LOOKING GLASS, FACETIME

The app is required. the app store you desire.
This app there is no fee!
Facetime to upload, your ready to roll,
Thanks to technology.

The device I see, a moment to be,
A means to view the world whole.
The phone to grasp, technology a task,
Communicate is just one of my roles.

The device to chose, to win or lose,
Whether iPhone or Android still rules.
The ability to converse, use of words,
To communicate by any means is cool.

Dial a friend, a moment to spend,
A contact reaches out to touch.
A simple way, to connect today,
This moment it means so much.

Years that pass, a time to grasp,
When distances to great to call.
A face on the phone, a happier tone,
Viewing the emotions will resolve.

The camera to view, images to peruse,
Ability to chat no Wi-Fi is required.
The number to dial, may bring a smile.
Pick up the phone when you desire.

The phone a device, not cheap for the price,
The ability to be able to connect.
The power to store, information and more,
Loosing it is stressful do not forget.

MY FIRST COMPUTER, A KEYBOARD, AND A RIBBON

This class I remember, early days of September,
One class so vivid years ago.
Theater was set, these machines I regret,
Row of seats and tables flowed.

Seven rows were seen, students now green,
Grade nine my first class of the day.
This device had a cover, like no other,
With latches affixed on display.

The front of the room, a large screen loomed,
With letters, numbered keys in a row.
The ability to view, from back of the room,
The challenge sitting close to know.

The cover removed, my ability to peruse,
What this box now contained inside.
With all the keys blanks, understand no thanks,
A lapse of judgment and my pride.

As the teacher spoke, my thoughts awoke,
Ability to not having to write again.
My cursive writing lacked, this device now backed,
Never to be red marked sunk in.

This task at hand, memorizing still stands,
Each letter, number, in its exact row.
As I looked at the keys, this was a breeze,
In time I'd regret the rhythmic flow.

Fingers on the keys, all eight you'll agree,
A cumbersome task just the same.
The goal as perceived, a challenge agreed,
Fifty words a minute was insane!

As the days progress, my fingers even less,
My ability to type fifty words a minute.
With two fingers and a thumb, empathy would succumb,
Fewer mistakes my time would limit.

Typing of the keys, striking them with ease,
Letters contacting ribbon were displayed.
The hammer did strike, the noise unlike,
For mistakes the eraser now played.

Align the sheet, as the typing is neat,
Typing each sentence to the end.
The end of the line, carriage return time,
Dirty fingers a ribbon is done in.

The yardstick a tool, for unsuspecting fools,
Eyes in the back of your head required.
Remembering her breath, was certain death,
Getting close I had no desire.

By the end of the term, my fingers learned,
Wearing gloves to protest the back.
To this day, I still type this way,
At least I will not get smacked.

ALONG THE COTTAGE ROAD, SILVERBIRCH BEACH, NOW SILVERBIRCH ROAD

Georgian Bay clear waters are seen,
Shimmering down in blue and green.
Sandy shores with islands to view,
Time up here memories I once knew.

Driving down highway six near the end,
First right you make the road will lend.
The last stretch of road the cottage awaits,
Minutes from now anticipation awaits.

Silverbirch beach it was once known,
Cottage road the gravel road has grown.
Silver birch trees once lined the road,
Silver and white the road set a glow.

For upon the road so few have seen,
Giant has shown a different scene.
As you drive towards the hill,
Just look above the vision instilled.

Upon the trees laid in a row,
Ever so slowly, the drive you will know.
Peer up along the line of trees,
Drawbridge opens those who can see.

Peering along the road trees unfold,
Door is opened to welcome all those.
Up the rise the door now ajar.
And stays in place until you go far.

He welcomes all the ones he knows.
When you leave the drawbridge will close,
He guards this way his kingdom grows.
Each night the stars above glow.

THIS PLACE CALLED HOME

Perhaps a thought may bring a smile,
That special someone for a little while.
All the while may it bring even more,
That added touch it's worth looking for.

Words and thoughts and times alone,
The moment to ponder sometime to roam.
Spread your wings to find that place,
Cherish the memories in that inner space.

A beating heart and warm embrace,
A smile appears it cannot be replaced.
Within the words within just one,
It is to remember especially for some.

Share a feeling thoughts and dreams,
Sharing moments something to be seen.
When you return when you recall,
This place called home it's special above all.

With many friends and more than some,
Allison you're remembered and you will become.
As your smile, it's always there,
When you're around you always share.

As each moment, another arrives,
As each new day, another surprise.
With that thought the feeling appears,
A smile appears and so do tears.

For all my love a surprise for you,
This day has brought a change for you.
As the warmth may it be shared,
And with the hope it'll always be there.

The love and dreams a tender smile,
You've got the knack you've got the style.
With each passing day, you'll carry this within,
From here it starts Allison & Igor it begins.

LIFE IN A BOX OF CRAYONS REVEALED

The box is new the crayons all sharp,
Do I open the box and do my part.
All lined up in order and size,
Pristine in shape colour and disguise.

Do I use these crayons or not,
I hate to mess up a clean box.
Bright, perfect I hate the thought,
Leave them alone in the box.

Opening the box, the smell of new,
Crisp and sharp what should I do?
Each crayon I start to draw around,
Before I know it's, all wore down.

Each crayon shrunk the more I use,
Smaller the crayon is now abused.
The papers torn colour runs,
Crisp and clean its no longer fun.

A box of twelve a rainbow shared,
The box is empty dirty and bare.
Once a new crayons life was magic,
A crayons life is unbearably tragic.

Next time to remember to ask,
A larger box with sharpener attached.
Saving each colour in shape and sharp,
Before it's worn down and doing my part.

THE AIR IS THINNER UP THERE

How do I explain, what's in may brain,
For me just being three feet tall.
Everywhere I go, I am short, I know.
I hate being this small.

I climb up the stairs, it's tiring up there,
My room is on the third floor.
Winded I get and no respect,
My legs weren't made for this chore,

Each step I take, is it a mistake,
I'm the oldest of three somehow.
I try to explain and am lost in vain,
It's not fair for me even now.

Each step I rise, higher to the sky,
I take a break after fourteen steps.
I look up to the next, fourteen now left,
The second floor is the best.

Staring at the floor, one more is a chore,
The stairs are steep from here.
One at a time, my little legs climb,
A break more than halfway, I fear.

The final flight, my door is in sight,
My room is up at the top.
My hearts pounds, less air surrounds,
My room, my laundry I forgot.

I sit and think time to blink,
Walking to the window to gaze
Looking up at the sky and wondering why
The window is too high anyway.

AUTUMN IN BALA ...A LESSENED YEAR 2020

We rise to the chance, once more to dance,
To celebrate all that Bala still shares.
Three days each year, northern trek is near,
To remember this passion, we're all aware.

Thirty-seven years and on, yet we still belong,
For one year was dearly missed.
A journey has begun, for a life but one,
This life of Joanie's was her gift.

Together we are strong, a lifelong bond,
Yet one soul has embarked.
One chair still glows, the feeling flows,
A sign on the arm, friendship apart.

The lady in **red**, is heavenly blessed,
Our spiritual advisor is here.
The path we bare, a cross to share,
In silence we know she's near.

We stand and pray, together one day,
Sweet Joanie we'll reunite.
We must be strong, share her bond,
Everyday look towards her light.

For countless days, the jokes were played,
Tears of laughter still flowed.
Laughter was a part, enlightening her heart,
Candle jokes never ending she told.

Another year, we celebrate great cheer,
The festival of cranberries still flows.
A tradition we mark, each year to embark,
Together each year we grow old.

The shores of long lake, a moment a break,
A few days to take a breath.
Many years we taught, marking & distraught,
Northern folks graciously made we forgot!

Now a toast for, Bala our host,
The cooler days and a chance to unwind.
Together we look ahead, now bow our heads.
Drink up its time, that we shine.

BALA BY THE BAY...
TOGETHER AGAIN 2022

A moment we ponder, this place we wander,
The smell of autumn draws near.
Sights and sounds when friends are around.
A place new friend reappears.
For thirty plus years, this event draws us near,
Three days of wine song and good cheer.
These folks who partake, to have and forsake,
Thankful for us all blessed to be here.
The colour over time, memories of mine,
To recollect and express a moment to shine.
A place remains, the shield will reign,
The folks up here they will resign.
A special place that hard to replace,
These days each year moments begin.
The bridge to walk, a challenge to cross,
To hold one's breath to venture within.
Upon the rock these lines will trace,
The life of the land to capture and embrace.
Down by the water these trees of green,
Bending and twisting something to be seen.
To capture to cherish to photograph and respect,
To view, to pause, a chance to reflect.
To listen and ponder to wade by the shore,
To walk to explore to venture once more.
The mist rolls in, the cold grips with pain,
Summer forgotten and silenced by name.
The sights, sounds, nature abound,
For all is lost, one aspect is found.

Friends and family who gather near,
To share, laugh and toast to good cheer.
The bums of Bala, once lost now found,
Lest we not forget, retired teachers are round.
Sounds by the shore echoes once more,
Lives we've lost let's remember once more.
Friends & family now we recall,
To drink & dance cherish this fall.
As night closes in and sun will retire,
Turn up the music a dance to inspire.
To Joanie our queen her graceful finesse,
The lady in red is now heavenly blessed.

A MEANS TO WRITE IN VERSE

A way to describe, let the words decide,
The ability to write in verse.
Create a thought, my writing has brought,
Ideas created in a way to converse.

Many hours it seemed, in thoughts and dreams,
Words worth writing about to express.
The reader decides, a sense of pride,
Happiness, sadness, love, loss, death.

Expression through time, changes designed,
Drawing the reader into view.
Imagination, desire, still reaching higher,
Thoughts and ideas to pursued.

Looking at the past, a moment to grasp,
Time had changed over the years.
Simple tasks explained, technology reigned,
Life gets faster change is revered.

A final thought, this special time has brought,
My book of poetry is almost done.
Forty years to create, months to debate,
The love and support of my wife was just one.

FALLING SIGNS

Green once prominent the forests alive,
Warmer weather as the forest thrives.
Time to remember a warmer retreat,
Days of summer have all but ceased.

Leaves once green the lack of rain,
Autumn comes sooner so begins change.
Leaves of brown, yellow and green,
Falling signs as weather changes its scene.

Skies have darkened cooler days lead,
End of summer as autumns ahead.
Lost is the humidity, cooler air arrives,
Sun, clouds reign as moisture thrives.

The air is cooler the temperature changed,
Summer is all gone it's never the same.
The sun now sets earlier each day,
Autumn is upon us and changes this way.

I gaze into the forest, I see a change,
Leaves on the trees have begun to fade.
Bark on the trees have darkened over time,
The leaves blossomed with colour falling signs.

The yellows, oranges, mixing in with red,
The colour and hue have now bled.
Loss of time for summer once seen,
Autumn approaches and a painter's dream.

Each day it seems the struggle to be seen,
The leaves have fallen far fewer are green.
Soon one day the trees will be bare,
Snow will arrive another season to share.

TRADITIONS, THE CHANGING TIMES AT BALA

The winds blew cold a sign of rain,
Up here in Bala no one complains.
The changing times for Bala retreats,
The rising costs for traditions defeats.

The connection to this special place,
Through the years memories replaced.
Looking back to a simpler time,
A weekend away happiness shined.

A driving force a spiritual pursuit,
A renewed experience following suit.
Breaking bread the love and support,
The Bala traditions are a driving force.

A retiring event making ends meet,
Pinching pennies an ongoing feat.
A place to stay the Bala-Hy change,
In the photographs memories remain.

A denial dance to kick up your heels,
The rhythm is lost a drink now reveals.
Sounds of laughter aching to the core,
Sharing from within is what Bala is for.

Between these walls the love is shared,
Photos taken calendars beware.
The autumn scene a colourful display,
We come up here a weekend away.

A button is chosen, the colour red,
Cranberry is celebrated shared instead.
Ten bucks a crack gets you in,
Rising signs fewer vendors within.

The bums of Bala a secret revealed,
Sharing the pact secret handshake concealed.
Fall is upon us another year is gone,
What of the future time marches on.

Faces places for many years we've come,
To celebrate friendship, teachers, everyone.
Over the years older we get we change,
Remember those in our hearts remain.

EARLY TO BED EARLY TO RISE, I THINK?

The sun arose the sky so blue,
The hour of six a restless brood.
A festive spirit a challenge for some,
Change of seasons not for everyone.

The fire is out a chill in the air,
Seeing your breath uneasiness fairs.
Pulling over covers or stay in bed,
Roll over go back to sleep instead.

Minutes pass the feeling to go,
Stepping down to the floor it's cold!
Waiting, watching how long to debate,
Thinking now with minutes to wait.

The sky was dark the clouds hung low,
Rain in the forecast, to stay or go.
The comfy feeling now warm in bed,
Get up for breakfast my voice inside said.

With mouths to feed one reason why,
Hunger inside the feeling just realized.
The duty for some a heathier chore,
Nourish the cells and dash out the door.

A sudden flash from the night before,
Drinking dancing a headache in store.
A glass of water so begins the day,
Headache powders takes the sting away.

Our time is short excitement to debate,
Cranberry festival weekend here awaits.
A fresh cup of coffee the aromas' sweet,
Breakfast for the early risers a real treat.

Walking outside to sun and blue skies,
Down to the bridge this moment realized.
Autumn splendor is now on display,
Capturing a moment before it goes away.

Time with friends a weekend to share,
Moments to ponder emotions to bare.
Bums of Bala another year has come,
Reminisce and remember blessings everyone.

THE MO I KNOW

The Mo I know is fast not slow,
She is cunning and special to know.
The Mo I know is thoughtful and brave,
She is understanding, kind & never afraid.

The Mo I know is a farmer at heart,
Growing red fruit sharing from her heart.
The Mo I know a teacher at best,
Guiding and thoughtfulness none the less.

The Mo I know is a Bala queen,
Photographing all by any means.
The Mo I know who cares for us all,
The knowledge instilled she never falls.

The Mo I know who creates still life,
Calendars through photographs brought to life.
The Mo I know beats a heart of gold,
Going to great lengths keeping her sights whole.

The Mo I Know nurturing at best,
Caring for her father with great respect.
The Mo I know this year she will be missed,
The fun, frolic laughter at Bala I'm pissed!

The Mo I Know facetime we shall see,
Sharing our thoughts when she can't be.
The Mo I know will rise to the top,
Fighting off this cold she'll never stop.

The Mo I know a great friend indeed,
Special to some over the years all agreed.
The Mo I know she's in our hearts,
A guardian angel is a few miles apart.

THE HALLOWEEN PUMPKIN WAS GREAT FULLY FILLED

The week was busy many mouths to feed,
Shopping for groceries filling the need.
Filling bags with Halloween candy galore,
300 plus bags many hands were a chore.

The challenge for mum was to overcome,
Five kids and costumes were just one.
Looking back on it how bars were large,
Chocolate and candy a better fix by far.

Three treats were placed and secured,
Placed in a bag lurking eyes did procure.
September arrived Halloween candy was bought.
Hidden and secured, or so mum thought.

In the storage room it was dark and cold,
Cunning kids searching high and low.
Hidden in the steamer trunk securely locked,
Creatively skilled or so mum thought.

A skeleton key, nail file, a bobby pin freed,
One less challenge was all we'd need.
Waiting until dark, dinner dishes all done,
Tiptoeing down to the cellar was great fun.

Each night we tried each taking a shift,
Scoring of Halloween candy getting our fix.
Halloween approaching pumpkins were few,
Not realizing we hadn't bought one, wouldn't do.

The hour of six fast approaching soon,
Mum's still at work no pumpkins, we're doomed!
Searching the garage, back and front stoop,
Sun now setting what now we're screwed.

Looking in the fridge no pumpkins in sight,
Searching for an alternative I had one bite.
It's small and round the size was right,
A yellow looking grapefruit out of sight!

With a marker in hand being precise,
Two eyes nose a smiling face just right.
Cutting a hole on top to view,
Creating the rest, no time to lose.

It was small yellow uniquely lit?
It did the trick in a pinch despite.
A candle was lit propped on display,
A sign read new pumpkin actor today.

Night was over the candy ran out,
The pumpkin reversed with a sign sold out.
Monday morning arrived my father was late,
His breakfast been stolen he was in a state.

Kellogg's K a treat no grapefruit in sight,
An empty shell the grapefruit got it right.
Five kids with smiles tummies filled,
Halloween pumpkin was grape fully fulfilled.

THE UGLY STICK A RHYTHMIC DELIGHT

Creatively designed, with one purpose in mind,
In ways and means to be of use.
Ugly stick appeared, its usefulness weird,
First thoughts to challenge its pursuits.

The long looking pole, its shape did control,
With its ability to tame the beasts.
Strength would prove, one cannot lose,
Its rhymical lines dazzled in its feats.

Unbreakable in its feats, exacting standards to meet,
Stringently following the will to know.
Tools of the trade, technology to wage,
Sourcing, creating will ultimately control.

The rod length inspired, exacting lines desired,
Over the years its expense was deserved.
The design and shape, uniquely a debate,
The technique would prove its worth.

Working within the constraints and few complaints
Fine improvements over the years its worth
Its length would disprove, flexibility did prove,
Its rigid and flexible did prove it worked

Novice or expert its not what they'd expect,
From tip to end the flexibility was proved.
The ugly stick was born, to challenge be warned,
This rod is determined one cannot lose.

With implements attached the ugly stick lacks,
Searching for the sweet spot to strike.
A spinning reel set fighting a trophy the best,
The ugly stick and its rhythmic delight.

NUTS

How to describe what I see inside,
My brain was never the same.
Thoughts invoked my mind awoke,
Some days I never complained.

This feeling within sometimes it wins,
Some days I never ask why.
Go with the flow, maybe never to know,
My ability to never reason to try?

A sensation I feel, is often real,
Sharing with others can be cruel.
Keeping close to home, somewhere to roam,
Caring, perhaps just being a fool.

The voices within, outside they begin,
Question within no answer why?
Hours I debate, sometimes I cannot wait,
My ability the hunger inside thrives.

Voice in my head, the feeling inside lead,
My will being one finally agreed.
The hours to wait time to debate,
The pain inside there is a need.

Giving into desire, reaching higher,
The hunger within needs to be fed.
I look for relief in the cupboard a need,
This moment inside I really dread.,

The view from here, the benefits near,
The decision which does it take.
The container chosen; sensation now frozen,
In the end my decision to make.,

Directions to read, understanding the need
The final answer one must take.
The lid now removed, medication will prove,
Peanuts, cashew's, pumpkin, sesame seeds forsake.

LOSING MY MARBLES

Staring into space no sense of being,
Looking inside something, I am seeing.
No sign of life, yet something stirs,
Lost inside still uttering few words.

Looking, searching, reasoning why,
Wondering where to go, wanting to die.
The hours each day still unknown,
Waiting and watching far from home.

Under the bed in darkness where to go,
Hiding in the corner wanting to know.
Asking a question who do I ask?
Lost in my thoughts unable to grasp.

Small yet round and smooth to the touch,
A game with friends means so much.
The aggie, immie, alley large and small,
Colourful objects a game of it all.

Hidden from sight nowhere to turn,
Lost forever thoughts of concern.
Within my brain thinking too long,
Loosing my marbles where they have gone.

With bonker, boulder, shooter, and thumper
Smasher, cats' eye, tom bowler and plumper
Boulder, masher, giant and dobber
There's popper, crock, and dobbert

*I am the Mibster and have my taw ready,
Into the ring the field calm and steady.
Striking the duck sometimes I lose,
The winner in the end keeps the bumboozer.*

*Cool shapes and sizes spherical and round,
Colours so intricate creativity is found.
Searching within the warm feeling remains,
Losing my marbles and finding them again.*

LOOKING AT SHEET OF WHITE PAPER?

Within this sheet an image appears,
Surrounded by its edges, faint yet near.
The wall of white, is all that it is,
Looking closer, curiosity forbids.

Fixated on the sheet, no image is seen,
What am I looking at, is this a dream?
The imagination is created now within,
Searching the sheet, the mystery begins.

Snow is falling all around is white,
Polar bear sleeping, just out of sight.
The flashlight is dead, no way to see,
Walking closer, a sense of intrigue.

How far to walk, how far to go,
This wall of white, no one knows.
My eyes are open, I cannot see,
Am I dreaming or a harsh reality?

Down on all fours, afraid to move,
Searching for the image, win or lose.
A light shining down I cannot see,
Straining my eyes hesitation leads.

Following the path, the way is unclear,
A voice in the distance faint I can hear.
Edging closer and my ability to see,
With eyes open there's nothing to see.

The breathing is heavy the closer I get,
Not seeing in the snow, no regrets.
Suddenly it stops my heart starts to race,
Lying on the ground the motion hesitates.

Waiting and wondering what happens now,
Slowing my heartbeat scared to death now.
The bears move slowing suddenly he stopped,
Wandering away my fear did not.

Light of the moon break through the snow,
The wind-blown terrain, little to know.
Turning back the direction from where I came,
Leaving the place was never the same.

Within the mind the eyes can believe,
A piece of white paper imagination sees.

BED BUGS

I waited and wondered for a place to sleep,
Laying my head on a, long-awaited treat.
The Inn chosen many miles on the road,
Finally arriving and my eyes to close.

The cover was drawn the sheets cleaned,
Soon to bed and a cozy place to dream.
Room temperature set just 16 degrees,
The night was dark I needed some ZZ's.

My phone set to charge laptop in bed,
Choosing to watch a movie instead.
Pulling back the sheets I was surprised,
Small dark lumps lying, I almost died.

Turning the light on searching for a cause,
Putting on my spectacles see what it was.
Tiny little objects circling the bed,
Looking closer to be examined instead.

Calling the front desk, waiting in disgust,
Wanting an answer, I was in a rush.
Long hours on the road, tempers flared!
Overtired yelling profanity I began to swear.

Bed bugs uncovered alone in my bed,
Where did they come, anger lead.
Tiny little shapes with a contoured look,
Volkswagen beetles surprise! you looked.

JUST A MATTER OF LINES FROM STILL TO LIFE

With an idea in mind, try to define,
The image that stirs within you.
Your ability to create, ideas you make,
This image that you hold true.

A challenge for some, to overcome,
To create and ability to sketch.
Following the lines, reveals over time,
Patience, a picture, nothing less,

A grid, that defines, image in the lines,
The idea takes center stage.
With preliminary lines, the image designs,
Countless hours you wage.

Simple lines, are pure, sometimes obscure,
Within the mind the image stirs.
Images created, shading now debated,
The ability to draw without words.

Within the theme, your colour scheme,
A pencil, pastels, or a lump of coal.
The device of choice, creates your voice,
With the tools you have the control.

Time to compare, time to share,
The image finally true to life.
Erase or enhance, a final glance,
A matter of lines creates still to life.

SEARCHING FOR BURIED TREASURE, X MARKS THE SPOT

Autumn is in full force, following its course,
Leaves had changed from green to red.
Now on this path, an old house I passed,
Nearing the porch peering inside instead.

Walking up to the door, a broken board,
Stepping lightly as the board broke.
Removing the board, beneath the floor,
Small metal box thoughts invoked.

Brushing away the leaves, a sense of intrigue,
Sitting on the stoop to open this box.
Looking both ways, hesitation weighs,
Wiping away debris revealing a lock.

Studying the box, and rusty old lock,
The image was faint and concealed
Searching for a key, skeleton type I'd need,
What's inside would be revealed.

Swiss army knife in hand, having a plan,
The hasp was secured with a tiny lock.
Many choices to reveal, the contents concealed,
Finding the key just one thought.

Many blades to choose, one cannot lose,
Trying each one, which one to pick.
Deciding which to try, patience on my side,
Small slot screwdriver was the trick.

Wrapped up tight, struggling to fight,
Layers of paper soon revealed.
A linen cloth, strange markings and cross,
Within the box a tiny map concealed.

Leaving the home, wandering on alone,
Figuring out the clues to the treasure
Strange markings exposed, landmarks arose,
Searching out the clues by every measure.

Following the path, I never looked back,
The journey to find the other side.
Light shone down, the path easier I found,
Narrowing trail shrinking in size.

The sky was dark, on my walk embarked,
The trail I followed to a fork.
Up over the rise, to the blue green skies,
Should I go back or move forth....

THE TRAIL FOR BURIED TREASURE, PART II

As night began the sky closed in,
Searching for a place to stay warm.
Climbing the rise, exposed roots would decide,
A footing and branches to conform.

Clouds rained down soaked through I found,
Drenching to my core to the bone.
Searching for cover, a grove like no other,
Looking for a place to call home.

Stand of trees entwined branches and leaves,
A carved-out cave appeared.
Small twigs and bark, the fire's warmth embarked,
Lighting a fire, eerie feeling neared.

Watching the light glowing with life,
Warmth now flowing inside.
Howling in the night winds whistling tonight,
Flickering of intrigue will decide.

Morning sun did rise hidden by disguise,
The fog hung heavy and low.
The chill of cold a feeling forbode,
Venturing outside now feeling exposed.

Studying the map with clues to track,
Adventure for treasure would begin.
With a compass and map, my ability to track,
The knowledge and terrain set in.

A challenge for some to overcome,
Deciphering clues on the map.
Symbols and shapes, the intelligence it takes,
Creativity and searching still attracts.

The trail aligned, the waters edge I'd find,
With a canoe and paddle to the stream.
Along the rivers edge, thick brush soon leads,
Depth of the water now on foot it seems.

A forest of vines, discouraged I did find,
Inching closer each step carefully chosen.
A rocky crest, was treacherous at best,
Reaching the base of a cliff was frozen

An etching on the rock, faded symbol worn off,
The map and the clue now revealed
Trail weaved a path, up the rock face at last,
A hole in the rock the parchment concealed

Following the clues, to a rock face viewed,
The etched face of the tinman shined.
Climbing the rock face, each step to debate.
A key in the clue set in a rhyme.

The final step, slippery rocks no regrets,
Stepping carefully so as not to fall.
The snow cover hills, the cold grip a chill,
The melted river of snow layers evolves.

Scouring the rivers edge, wading in the water lead,
The melting glaciers waters biting cold.
Plunging in the depth, a shinny object no less,
A vice that gripped my frozen soul.

*Wading to the shore, warming my body to its core,
A fire to rejuvenate and decipher each clue
Retrieving the artifacts, collection the facts,
Solving the treasure map and the answers too.*

MY IMAGINATION WENT AWAY

Dark is the night, excitement did ignite,
A feeling I cannot describe.
There is something within, my mind begins,
A feeling inside me has died.

Looking up at night, seeing the moonlight,
Hoping to have a nice dream.
Waking with the sun, losing track just one,
I have forgotten how to dream.

I close my eyes, hard as I try,
Thinking is too much work.
My crayon in hand, stick people just stand,
No ideas ever seem to work.

I remember when, talking with my friend,
My imagination was so cool.
The ideas in my brain, never did I complain,
Neat stuff was my golden rule.

I look and stare, a blank page everywhere,
Nothing is coming to my brain.
I talked with my folks, in a letter I wrote,
I will never be the same.

I close my eyes, hard as I try,
To remember what it was like.
Looking at my ride, two wheels by my side,
Just as me riding my bike.

Many months it seems, nothing to dream,
The days seems all the same.
I've given up hope, trying to cope.
My imagination has gone away.

SEARCHING FOR WINTER

Sounds of winter have come and gone,
And the freshly fallen snow.
The challenge to ski, it's been too long,
The signs may never show.
As it been the runs are green,
Sights of winter are lost,
Yet all around the warmth we've seen,
Winter, we haven't crossed.

As each night, we pray for snow,
Each day it seems to rain.
Signs of winter are rarely cold,
Skiing we'll have to refrain.
All our time and money spent,
Just a few days of fun.
The money earned, every red cent,
Less patient we've all become.

All around spring is here,
In winter it used to snow.
At time we froze just to ski,
These days, it's hard to know.
Weather reports we used to trust,
Smiles all they would bring.
We wait and wonder in disgust,
Observing this thing called spring.

Trying to ski we do in vain,
The snow is almost gone.
Conditions they're always the same,
Winter now has moved on.
Hours we spend each year,
Further north to find snow.
Waiting in line frustration here,
Rising equipment costs grows.

November arrives, cold and snow,
To have the weather change.
December returns seeing winter go,
The climate is never the same.
Maybe one day the cold will arrive,
The smiling faces will return.
As for now we look at they sky,
Snow for this we've earned.

FRIESEN FAMILY

Thanks to FriesenPress for seeing this through,
Working through the process it's beneficial too.

My publishing consultant his wisdoms praised,
Ironing out details on my fixed income wage.

With technical assistance organizing each page,
Systematically and coordinating poems by day.

The editor diligently reviewing my manuscript,
Thousands of words grammatically, nothing missed.

Proofreading my manuscript in retrospect,
Creatively, improving, expecting nothing less.

About the author many questions were asked.
Pinpointing and the review were within her grasp.

My publishing specialist coordinating my book,
Making the necessary changes, nothing overlooked.

Guidance through emails, chatting on the phone,
Step by step instructions you're never alone.

My designer coordinator from cover to cover,
Analytically creating my book like no other.

A few months from now the books will arrive,
Opening the box, a published poet thrives.

From cover to cover many years to write,
Reading each poem an author's insight.

*Through the process from inception to print,
Finally, being published was worth every cent.*

THE NEXT STEP, VIEWING FROM THE OTHER SIDE, PUBLISHED

The day arrived the moment I knew,
The package was delivered excitement grew!
Years to create assemble and write,
The final products were in my sights.

A knock at the door the postman smiled,
Here is your delivery, struggling awhile,
The brown box inside, the book awaits.
Finding the scissors, hesitation debates.

Slowly the scissors guide along the seem,
Cutting ever so slowing, years it's been.
A slit at the end, one flap is done,
One by one three seams, the final one.

Flap now opened the fragrance arrived,
The fresh printed books aroma inside.
Forty years writing the dream realized,
Countless hours deliberating the final prize.

The view from here, a moment a thought,
The emotions stirred feelings stopped.,
Many years to create the story now lies,
In theses pages reading soon realized.

A part of my life, all aspects seen,
Emotions of writing one final dream.
Staring at the cover, looking deep within,
Vision now realized nurturing begins.

Opening the cover looking at the name,
Reading the dedication thoughts remain.
One who inspired my ability to write,
Cannot enjoy this part of my life?

Stories of others I have encountered in life,
Knowing they played a small part ignites.
One whom I hold dear in my heart,
In the beginning we were never apart.

Back of the book the cover reveals,
Newfoundland once visited history concealed.
Another Time & Place this book reveals,
Writer Silverghost the penname he's real.

The book of poetry a memoir in verse,
Enjoy reading hidden gems in words.
Within these chapters the author reveals,
Friends and family, these feelings are real.

My coach, a mentor and loving wife,
Since we met and every day of my life.
Encouraging this adventure teaching dawned,
A financial wizard whose wisdom spawned.
My first book of poetry it may be my last,
Writing each day inspiring and laughs.
Humbled to the core published by name,
Never forgetting the ongoing support remains.

Printed in Canada